God Within Her

100 Inspiring Devotionals
For Women by Women

Stonegate Publishing Co., Inc.
Lubbock 2020

Stonegate Publishing Co., Inc.
3119 112th Street
Lubbock, TX 79423
Vivianbkeith@gmail.com

To my loving mother Veva Bustillos, my wonderful children Miguel and Marisa, and my amazing grandchildren Riley, Micaela, Genna, Andrew, Macy, and Olivia.

"God is within her, she will not fall;
God will help her at break of day."

Psalm 46:5

Foreword

If you want to learn how to experience a breakthrough in your life and how to overcome in the areas the enemy seems to attack you the most, I highly recommend the study of this excellent devotional book for women by women, together with your daily Bible reading.

As I read through this devotional book that my dear friend, Vivian Bustillos Keith, was inspired to compile, I felt like I was meeting these ladies personally and receiving great insight and encouragement from their testimonies and counsel.

You will enjoy reading each devotional and I am sure you, too, will be encouraged and challenged to trust God in every circumstance.

There are so many thoughts that are constantly flooding our minds and senses that we must schedule quality time to edify and feed ourselves spiritually. If we don't, we will end up frustrated and open to the constant attacks of the enemy. I would like for you to really pay attention to what the Holy Spirit wants to teach you through the counsel that is contained in this book.

I have learned that it is possible to live in a dysfunctional, chaotic home and still be under God's blessing when there is one person in that home willing to stand in the gap for that family. In my home, my mother was that one person. That is why I'm a devoted believer, and like my sister in Christ, Vivian, and the other authors, imparting wisdom to other women through this devotional book.

Don't wait to begin to enjoy the blessings that God has already ordained and prepared for you! Develop a keen interest to know Him and experience His presence.

Dr. Iris Delgado
Author of the Charisma book series: *Satan You Can't Have My Children; Satan You Can't Have My Marriage; Satan You Can't Have My Miracle;* and *Satan You Can't Have My Promises.*

Preface

It has been a dream of mine to put together a devotional book for women by women. I know that God planted this idea in my heart but I never knew when I would have time for the project. However, in 2019, I heard God say, "Now is the time."

Thus, I reached out to some of my sisters in Christ and invited them to join me on this journey. These amazing friends are women of all ages, women of color, single, married, divorced, professionals ranging from college professors, teachers, business women to women in ministry.

I know these women. They are vibrant…courageous… beautiful…and most of all they love serving the Lord. Their devotionals contain personal stories and words of encouragement for women of all walks of life. As I compiled and edited these devotionals, each of them ministered to me. They are written from the heart and I pray they will provide hope and joy to you.

You will note that each woman has a different writing style – a personal and spiritual biblical insight that makes this book special. To name a few, you will be moved by "He's Calling You" by Elsa Guajardo...be convicted by "Our Belief Meter" by Sharon Shelton...rejoice with "My New Faith" by Maimuna Mbeh...and chuckle with "I Love Grackles" by Julia Lutz.

I want to give a special thanks to Deena Shelton who assisted me with the title of this book.

Also, to my wonderful husband Bill who helped with the editing and let me use his desktop after my laptop crashed! We worked many long hours far into the night. We laughed, we prayed and we ate a lot of snacks! He became my hero in my time of need.

I would also like to thank the following people who made this dream of mine come true:

Jim Hardin, a retired journalist/columnist and personal friend who put in countless hours helping with the editing. He was a lifesaver!

Ernest Silver, a graphic design professional, who has always performed outstanding work for our publishing company.

Rebekah Wilkins-Pepiton, a creative graphic artist, who created a book cover that is dramatic and profound. I couldn't have asked for a better design.

Dr. Iris Delgado, a well-known author and the President of Crowned with Purpose, a ministry dedicated to helping and mentoring others, wrote the foreword. She and her husband, Dr. John Delgado, travel the globe together sharing the message of restoration and training leaders for the work of the Kingdom of God.

And last but not least to all my prayer warrior friends, your constant support and prayers helped me complete this project.

All glory and honor to Jesus Christ, our Lord and Savior.

~Vivian Bustillos Keith

Hidden No Longer

Alaina Strait

When the woman (with the issue of blood) realized she couldn't hide any longer she came and fell trembling at Jesus' feet.
Luke 8:47 (TPT)

Have you ever had a moment when you got up early to have some quiet time with the Lord before the day began? As you read the Word, God suddenly spoke so loudly that you felt He had been reading your mail. You stopped and grabbed a pen to journal what He was saying to you.

I had one of those moments a few weeks ago. As I read Luke 8:47, the phrase "…she couldn't hide any longer…" jumped off the page. I felt God say to me, "You can relate to that."

In my heart, I said, "Lord, you are right. I can."

For so long, I tried to fade into the background. Hurts and scars in my life had so affected me that I wanted to just keep to myself. That way I would feel safe and not hurt again.

Like the woman in this Scripture, God called me out of the crowd. Amazingly, He placed people in my life and used them to recognize and unveil my gifts and talents. I realized that God didn't create me to be alone but to boldly be the woman He created me to be. I believed that during this time of seclusion, God healed me spiritually.

Have you been hiding from the amazing things God has called you to do? God sees you! You are a daughter of the King! Take your rightful place with Jesus and determine to move forward! Be brave! Take one step at a time. Before you know it, you will be where He created you to be.

Father, help us have lives that always shine brightly for You, and let the gifts and talents You have placed in us be used for your glory. Amen.

Help Has Arrived

Allison Wolfe Cunningham

*I lift my eyes up to the hills – where does my help come from? My help comes
from the Lord, the Maker of heaven and earth.*
Psalm 121:1-2 (NIV)

Healthy living is a buzz word in our culture. Everywhere you
turn someone tells you what to eat or not eat, how to exercise, where
to shop, what to buy, etc. There are pills, vitamins and oils galore!
Whatever problem you have, minor ailment or inconvenience,
there is a product for you.

We live in an information age where technology has made it
very easy to self-prescribe, self-identify and self-help. The problem
with this is there are so many voices saying many different things.
Much of what is advertised as "good for you" is not driven by
sincere interests or what is best for you. Who then do you trust?

When you know Christ, your resources are limitless! His power,
wisdom and help are available to you. Do you need a strategy for
how to handle a situation? Do you need healing? Do you need
peace? Jesus is your source. He is able to give you everything you
need.

Your answer may come through a supernatural provision or He may lead you to utilize the resources of the natural world we live in. Jesus is alive and the Holy Spirit is your helper!

Lift your eyes from your needs and gaze on the One who can sustain you in every situation. If He can create something out of nothing and tell the ocean where to stop, He can certainly take care of you. All the products and information of this world are merely resources but God is our source!

No matter what season of life you are in, how big or small your problem; no matter if it is physical, emotional or relational, the Lord is your help! His ways are sure. His wisdom supreme. His direction is gentle. His guidance comes through peace. He is motivated by love and His answers are wrapped in hope. Receptivity is the key.

Jesus, give me courage to trust You as my source, knowing You are willing and able to change, create, redirect and do the miraculous in my life for the glory of your name, amen.

God Meets Us Where We Are

Andrée Elliott

And it happened the same night that the LORD said to him [Gideon],
Arise! Go down to the Midian camp, for I have delivered it into your hand.
But if you fear to go down, go with Purah your servant down to the camp,
and you will hear what they are saying and afterward your hands will be
strengthened to go down to the camp.
Judges 7:9-11 (ONMB)

Notice how the Lord addressed Gideon. God knew that he had fear in his heart, but He did not condemn him for it. Instead, the Lord met him emotionally where he was by telling him what to do to be strengthened and filled with courage.

God's instructions to Gideon contrast with how He addressed Joshua when he was to lead the Israelites into the Promised Land after the death of Moses: "Have I not commanded you? Be strong! Be of good courage! Do not tremble! Do not be dismayed! For the Lord your God is with you wherever you go" (Joshua 1:9). The Lord did not address Gideon the same way He addressed Joshua; He knew what each one needed based on who they were.

Likewise, God knows *our* hearts; He addresses each of us

individually based on where we are in our walk with Him. As He did for Gideon, so He does for us: He meets us where we are and gives us what we need in order to accomplish that which He has called us to do. Because the Lord has the same disposition towards us as He had toward Gideon, we can relax, trust and rest in Him.

We need only to keep our eyes on the Lord and to obey Him. The onus is on Him to bring to fruition the results of following and obeying Him. Just as God treated Gideon and Joshua each uniquely, so will He treat you and me. He knows us and He loves us!

Father, I thank You for meeting me where I am. Thank you, Lord, for your faithfulness and for causing me to grow in You. Help me to trust You more! In Jesus' name, amen.

Hearing God

Beth Collins

But he who prophesies speaks edification and exhortation
and comfort to men.
1 Corinthians 14:3 (NKJV)

How do you hear from God? Furthermore, how do you recognize His voice when He speaks to you?

Do you just know it's God or feel in your heart that it's Him? Honestly, it can be a little confusing and overwhelming!

The Apostle Paul instructs us to minister to those around us with words of comfort and encouragement. The main purpose for hearing God in our everyday lives is not just to know what job to take or which house to buy, rather it is for strengthening others.

Unfortunately, we as a society have become self-centered. We live in a social-media driven world that attempts to define success for us, and we can forget that the Gospel is the main purpose for life. We are to seek and save those who are lost.

Our purpose as wives, mothers and friends is to ask God this question daily, "Who do you want me to encourage today and how can I partner with You in your Kingdom?" Then simply wait for

His answer.

He speaks to us through the Holy Spirit. I have found that when I am in need, He comes and speaks to me about the personal concerns on my heart and He will do that for you.

Ask Him today to give you a word of encouragement and comfort for your children, your husband and others around you.

Teach your children how to ask God questions, wait for His answers and write them down. Also teach them how to ask God for a word for someone else.

Hearing God should be as natural as breathing or eating. Satan wants us to believe it is impossible to hear from God and that He is silent. But be assured that God uses words to heal, to restore and to save!

Dear God, help me to take time today to clear my mind so that I can hear from You. I want to partner with You and your Kingdom. Give me words of comfort to speak to my family and to those who are broken and hurting. Amen.

In The Midst Of Pain

Brenda Telles

...and provide for those who grieve in Zion— to bestow on them a crown of beauty instead of ashes, the oil of joy instead of mourning, and a garment of praise instead of a spirit of despair. They will be called oaks of righteousness, a planting of the LORD for the display of his splendor.
Isaiah 61:3-4 (NIV)

Suffering is inevitable in this world. All of us, in one form or another, have had to face an illness, the loss of a loved one, injustice or, because of our own mistakes, have endured suffering. We can be assured that God is aware of our situation because He is an all-knowing, omnipresent God.

In the midst of my personal pain and despair of the loss of an adult child, I knew nothing but to run to the arms of God. I felt the character of God on display like no other time. He chose to hold, comfort and reassure me that He is who He says He is.

God is the author and finisher of our faith, and we must trust Him even when we don't understand.

God promised me in this Scripture a crown of beauty instead of ashes, the oil of joy instead of mourning and a garment of praise instead of despair. That is why I wear this promise on the tablet of my heart.

With that said, if you haven't already committed your life to the Lord, my prayer for you today is that you will ask Jesus into your heart and get rooted in His Word so that you, too, will know the beauty of His character and goodness through salvation.

Lord, when in the midst of trials, help me to keep You the center of my life that my eyes will be fixed on You even when things are beyond my understanding. As I run to You, may I view circumstances from your eternal perspective. Amen.

A House Well Built

Christine Lanton

*As for everyone who comes to me and hears my words and puts them into
practice, I will show you what they are like. They are like a man building
a house, who dug down deep and laid the foundation on rock. When a flood
came, the torrent struck that house but could not shake it, because it was well
built.*

Luke 6:47–48 (NIV)

I walk through the rooms of my house in ruins. It was a bit
startling to me how fast my kitchen was demolished. Granted, I
planned this remodel, but now as I see the walls and the concrete…
no signs of life…no pictures of family…a strange echo when I say
something…it is both depressing and confusing.

Of course, I remind myself that when this project is done, it
will be worth it. My house will be updated, bright and functional!
(My cabinets were a nightmare.) Still, the process is longer than I
expected. The cost has been high.

My sleep is disturbed and my daily routine is severely altered.
Without a working kitchen, I have to seek out food and water in
alternate places. It takes more energy and seems less satisfying in

a strange way.

The Lord has gently given me a visual of some hard times in my life – places where I thought all was lost and that there was nothing good that could come from this. In these times, there has to be a reservoir you can draw from.

My walk with Jesus during the good times helped me press through in the not-so-good times. I heard His Words and now I sit in the ruins and I must put them to practice.

Step by step, I make the hard decisions and press through until I see beauty come from the rubble. I know that God built my house well. I can face the emptiness that I feel now and focus instead on the Promise.

Lord, thank You for building my house both physically and spiritually, and reminding me that even in the dark and confusing times that my faith will not be shaken because You built my house well. Help me to hear your Word and obey it! In Jesus' name, amen.

Crafted For Christ

Dawana Quintana

For We are God's Masterpiece. He has created us anew in Christ Jesus, so we can do the good things He planned for us long ago.
Ephesians 2:10 (NLT)

Things that are handmade and crafted by artisans are of great value.

We are like that! Handmade and one of a kind, fashioned by the Master of all design. Each one of us has a uniqueness that sets us apart from all others while also having a likeness that draws others to us. That kind of workmanship can only be done by the Creator.

The same One who fashioned the universe also fashioned you. Every molecule of your molecular system was thought out by Him. Every hormone, too! What makes you tick...what makes you smile...what makes you breakout into dance – God designed all these things.

You truly are His masterpiece! But let's be real. We have sullied and marred our lives and we need to be created anew in Christ. He made us and knows just what we need to be artfully restored. He knows where our cracks are. He also knows just how to fill them!

Why does He even bother? Because each of His masterpieces was created with a purpose, each to be a part of a master plan. His desire is that all His renewed works of art draw in the others that need restoration thus creating a worldwide exhibition of His great love. His plan for your life is as unique as you are.

Some art will traverse the world from gallery to gallery and be seen by millions. Some will hang on a refrigerator door. They all have the same goal – to bring life and light to all who see. God made you! He loves you! He is always ready to make a repair if and when needed! His plan for you is good!

Father, today I choose to see myself as your masterpiece. I choose to allow You into any broken or cracked areas of my life to restore me. I know that You have a divine purpose for my life. Let my life reflect You, my Creator, to everyone who sees me. I am made by You and for You! Amen.

Heartbreak

DeAnna Lucas

But you, God, shield me on all sides;
You ground my feet, you lift my head high;
With all my might I shout up to God,
His answers thunder from the holy mountain.
Psalm 3:3-4 (MSG)

Have you ever had a broken heart? Ever felt at your lowest point in life and you were utterly alone? Wow, I could raise my hand right now and sheepishly admit that I've been there more than once.

I have felt true heartbreak. From a job that didn't work out that I knew was meant for me, a misunderstanding with a close friend and the devastating sting of rejection from the person I thought would be by my side forever. Yes, I have been there.

There are so many reasons people feel heartbreak. In my short twenty-four years I've experienced more than I thought I could handle. The problem was trying to deal with these emotions alone. Often, I pictured the Lord looking down from Heaven waiting for me to give up control and allowing Him to lead me.

It wasn't until a kitchen floor breakdown (we've all been there) that I had a beautiful revelation. The way I overcame this heartbreak was to realize that God was my comforter and protector. That is the best defense against a very real enemy that uses our vulnerability to cause us to doubt the Lord.

This Scripture became my mantra. The moment I wanted to blame God for my heartbreak, I began to praise Him for my healing.

He is my foundation, but especially in the unsteady atmosphere in this world.

Unfortunately, hurt happens. If we dwell in the pain, it will keep us there. It's when we decide to put our trust in God that determines how we come out on the other side of that hurt.

The heart of God is forgiveness and wholeness! If you are in the middle of a similar season, seek the heart of God and see the manifestation of His healing.

God, may I find myself in You. Lift my head and continue to mend my heart. Steady my emotions and allow me to find your joy and peace in my situations. Amen.

Speak The Word

Debbie Lucas

Death and life are in the power of the tongue and those who love it will eat its fruit.
Proverbs 18:21 (ESV)

Being a mom of four children has given me plenty of opportunities for teaching moments.

One of the most memorable was with my youngest daughter DeAnna who would wake up in the middle of the night with bad dreams and fear. Led by the Holy Spirit, I asked her to speak 2 Timothy 1:7: "God has not given me a spirit of fear, but of power, and of love and of a sound mind," and to continuously quote it.

When she realized the Bible actually said that fear is not from God, it took root in her heart, and her faith in what the Word said began to eradicate it.

Today, DeAnna is one of the most fearless young adults I know. How profound that one Scripture verse can change her life so dramatically.

No matter the situation, the Bible has something to say about every issue we face. God's Word is alive and will do what He says it will do. It will not return to Him void.

Today, my children will tell you that whenever they came to me with a problem, I would most likely ask them, "What does the Word say?"

Even after being a Christian for over thirty-five years I still remind myself of this truth.

While in the wilderness, what did Jesus do when Satan tempted Him? Every time he answered him with, "It is written."

By declaring the Word of God, mountains can be removed.

Lord, thank You for your living and powerful Word. Help me always to embrace it and keep your precepts in my heart. I pray that the Holy Spirit will guide me through every situation. If I have failed to seek your Word, show me my neglect and lead me back to "It is written."
In Jesus' name, amen.

Change The Right Thing

Deena Shelton

I knew you before I formed you in your mother's womb. Before you were born, I set you apart.
Jeremiah 1:5 (NLT)

How often do we get caught up thinking life would be better if we were different in some way? "If I could just be as popular and friendly as she is…" "If I could just not be so sensitive…" "If I could be as good a cook/party planner/mom/wife/friend…" It is tempting to believe that if we change that one thing, we would be happy.

But that is a lie that leads us into a pattern of being dissatisfied with ourselves. We compare ourselves to others (oftentimes the shiny internet version) and feel like our life pales in comparison. But that is not how God intended us to live! God told Jeremiah that he was known before he was formed and God had plans for him. Jeremiah's immediate response was that he was too young and did not know how to speak well, and God stopped him from using excuses about why he wasn't enough.

Could it be that some things we are trying to change could be used for Him? What if a quiet, shy demeanor is not a downfall, but a spirit that notices those who need to be seen? What if a sensitive spirit is not something to be hardened, but something that shows part of the nature of Jesus to others? What if the skills where we struggle are opportunities for connective humor with our families or for us to be an example of self-love and acceptance even though we don't have it all together?

Sometimes, God asks us to work on parts of ourselves that He wants to grow. Other times, we focus on changing things that are gifts from Him. Consider the thing you have identified you feel needs to change for you to be happy and ask God to change your heart.

Lord, You know my struggles better than I do, but I know You created me with purpose. Teach me how to use what You put in me to point people back to You. Amen.

Pay Close Attention

Diane Hawkins

Therefore, we must pay much closer attention to what we have heard, lest we drift away from it.
Hebrews 2:1 (ESV)

A few years ago, my brother served as a corpsman on the Naval ship USS Wasp. The ship travelled from country to country, port to port in service to America.

Though the ship often anchored at port, there were times it would park in the ocean. The water around them stretched for miles and it was imperative they drop anchor to prevent the ship from drifting in the open waters. If a ship neglected to drop anchor, it could find itself miles from its original destination.

The writer of Hebrews cautions readers to "pay attention" to Scripture, so that they won't be like an unanchored ship and drift, because it can be difficult to sense a gradual change. Sometimes those that drift away may be unaware they have drifted until they are miles from where they began.

As women of God, we must ground ourselves in His Word to prevent drifting. Circumstances of life can cause us to question and lose our faith. We hear questions/comments voiced from those around us daily: "What is Christianity about?" "Christians are a bunch of hypocrites!"

In Galatians 2:12-14, Paul rebuked Peter for drawing back from the Gentiles when the Jews came from Jerusalem. Peter drifted due to his fear of the Jews. Paul recognized the drift and called him out on it. He gave him an anchor and set Peter back on the right course.

As I serve God, I do not want to choose my own way and do my own thing with the belief that I am not prone to drift. I must stay anchored in the Scriptures. I have great need of a Savior who has paid the price that I was unable to pay.

Yes, there are times that just like Peter, I fail to obey as I should but His grace looks past failure and into faith. I have a Savior and he calls me to repentance and anchors me in His Word so that I will not drift.

Father thank You that You provide the anchor to our souls and call us to "Come back!" when we drift. Amen.

He's Calling You

Elsa Guajardo

For God so loved the world that He gave His only begotten Son, that
whosoever believeth in him should not perish,
but have everlasting life."
John 3:16 (KJV)

Every Easter season, our church celebrates the Lord's Supper in a special way.

Typically, the church is open several hours on Good Friday evening. People can enter the sanctuary quietly, pick up a guide with instructions, read Scripture and privately partake of the bread and wine. It is a moment of reflection and one-on-one time with the Lord.

I remember the first time I partook of this special celebration. I was overcome with emotion. I felt the Lord's presence so strongly, which reminded me of the great sacrifice He had made for me because He loved me. I also felt the anguish and pain He suffered for me.

I could in that moment see His face, filled with pain and disappointment, not in what was happening to Him but, perhaps, in the people who let Him down. I realized at that moment that my sins made this happen. But in the same instance, I felt His loving arms wrapped around me like a parent with their child when they had done something wrong.

It was assuring to me that in spite of all my failures, my missteps, my bad decisions and choices, He would do it all over again because He loves me.

Those moments celebrating the greatest gift mankind has ever been offered will always be special because, you see, this isn't just a story someone told. It isn't a fairy tale. The Bible, God's Scripture to us, gives us all the details of that event. All we have to do is believe in Him, accept His gift and be forever saved.

WOW! How simple is that?

I pray today that if you have not accepted this gift Christ offers you that you will stop this instant and accept Him as your Savior. His Word says, "…that whosoever believeth in Him should not perish, but have everlasting life." Don't wait. He is calling you today.

Lord, your Word says in Revelation 3:20, "Behold, I stand at the door and knock. If anyone hears my voice and opens the door, I will come in to him and dine with him, and he with me." Today I want to open the door of my heart and invite You to come into my life. Amen.

Faith Of A Child

Helen Lynn

By His stripes we are healed. Isaiah 53:5 (NKJV)

My youngest daughter Rebecca was our miracle baby. She was quite ill and unable to digest food properly. Furthermore, we were told that the prospects for her future were grim. By the time she was two years old, she existed on a very limited diet of less than five basic foods and baby formula.

From a very young age, we taught her to believe the Word of God and she learned to develop her own faith. At the age of three, Rebecca went to the nursery on Sunday mornings and attended Sunday night services with me. At the conclusion of the services, our church opened the altars for anyone that wanted prayer and it was not uncommon for Rebecca to run to the altar.

On a particular Sunday night, a pastor asked Rebecca if she knew any nursery rhymes. Of course, she knew many. He then looked at us and said, "If she can memorize a nursery rhyme, then she can memorize Scripture."

That night he taught her three Bible verses that would build a foundation for healing in her life. He instructed her to repeat these Scriptures out loud every time she had to take any medicine.

As she took her medicine several times a day, she would say, "By His stripes, I am healed" (Isaiah 53:5); "No sickness or disease can come near my house" (Psalm 91:10); and "It is my desire that I prosper and be in health even as my soul prospers" (3 John 1:2).

Rebecca not only spoke these truths to herself but to others as well. She believed what God said about healing and faithfully repeated these verses. When she was six years old, the Lord miraculously healed her.

The Lord heard Rebecca's prayers and He hears yours as well. All you need is the faith of a child!

Gracious God, your Word brings life when we speak and believe it. Thank You that Jesus paid for it all and by His stripes we are healed. Amen.

Facing Evil

Holly Frank

For the eyes of the Lord are on the righteous,
and His ears are open to their prayers;
But the face of the Lord is against those who do evil.
1 Peter 3:12 (NKJV)

Do you ever feel like God is watching you? It's the alert sense of having His eyes on you, or maybe just the smile of His good pleasure. We have comfort that He SEES us and His eyes are ON us.

There is also strength in knowing when we call on Him, He is ready to hear our voice and is open to what we're asking.

Now, think of how your face can look tense with a set jaw and your eyes go from wide and bright to slits staring. When you get that look, your whole being knows that something is just off, and that something is known about you and what you're doing.

Peter gives us a stark difference in how God interacts with the righteous versus the evil. There's security in knowing that God has the backbone to look at evil, shift His weight and put His whole face toward it.

Could we stop for a moment and accept the truth that He is a good Father, looking at His creation in love and absorbing the reality that they have chosen evil?

Let's direct our intent and prayers to those who do evil that they will look up and meet that firm gaze! May they realize the fullness of the One who is staring at them.

May evil shake in the face of goodness and uprightness when those who do evil join the righteous and see their own prayers fully heard. What a shift that will be in that moment! What a relief for that soul to go from grabbing to having. Only the Lord our God could do that.

Father, rescue those deceived by evil. Be faithful to press out of them all the chaos they stir up. If they step into doing evil, let them notice that they are seen and opposed – and may it save them from the chaos of pulling down their own lives. May we all choose to call out for what we need and happily wait for it. Amen.

Mountains Of Life

Janie Peña

*For the mountains may be removed and the hills may shatter, but my
lovingkindness will not be removed from you. And my covenant of peace
will not be shaken, says the Lord
who has compassion on you.
Isaiah 54:10 (NAS)*

On a recent trip to Europe, I was blessed to see the Swiss
Alps for the first time. Driving through the mountains was awe-
inspiring as I witnessed the majesty of God's handiwork.

This Scripture from Isaiah tells us three things 1) Mountains
may shake or be removed but God's love will not be removed;
2) His covenant of peace will not be shaken; and 3) He has
compassion on us.

The immensity of the Alps was inescapable and I could not
help but reflect on what these mountains have witnessed through
the centuries including times of peace, times of turmoil and times
of war.

The same can be said of the people we see around us every
day. We may see the individual but we often do not know the

"mountains" they are struggling with in their daily lives. Perhaps it is a health challenge; the loss of a loved one; or dealing with shattered dreams.

All of these "mountains" seem immense to the person in the midst of the challenge. So, what do we say to those struggling? As sisters in Christ, we can share the assurance of His Word which tells us "the mountains may shake or be removed but His love for us will not be removed."

Unlike the Alps which can be seen from many miles away, there are some "mountains" we often try to hide from the world. These are the most difficult to acknowledge and resolve, yet we must deal with them if we seek peace.

There are challenges such as letting go of regret; giving or accepting forgiveness to ourselves and others; and struggling with the "why me Lord" moments we all face in life. Yet, again, the Scripture provides the truthful and comforting response – His covenant of peace will not be shaken.

While the mountains in our life may not always be as beautiful as the Alps, they, too, can inspire and help put into perspective the assurance of God's promise and compassion.

Help me, Lord, to never forget the promise You have made to us of your lovingkindness and assurance of peace and compassion. Amen.

Who Defines You?

Jenn Eze

*And all spoke well of him and marveled at the gracious words that were
coming from his mouth. And they said, "Is not this Joseph's son?"*
Luke 4:22 (ESV)

Who and what do you allow to define you?

In Luke 4, we see Jesus openly declare His identity according
to the Heavenly Father. Then we see others come right behind
Him and try to define Him according to His earthly father Joseph.

There was certainly nothing wrong with them identifying
him as Joseph's son. After all, Joseph was a good man and not a
criminal or outcast.

But a vital point that this Scripture teaches us is that we should
refuse to accept any identity that is not God-given, whether it be
good or bad.

Your parents, husband or children do not define you.

Your ministry, business or career do not define you.

Your beauty or intellect do not define you.

Your past or future do not define you.

Yes, it is true that as believers we begin to see good fruit in all of the above-mentioned areas, but not until *after* we have solidified the foundation of our identity in God.

Our identity is like the soil and without it being rich with revelation of being God's beloved, we will not grow truly good fruit.

Is the soil dependent upon the fruit that grows in it? No. Rather the fruit is dependent upon the soil. In the same way, the fruit of your life is dependent upon being rooted in beloved identity.

Refuse to settle for a "good" identity – you are who God says you are.

If you are struggling to find who God says you are, recite these declarations: "I am the righteousness of God in Christ Jesus" (2 Corinthians 5:21); "I am no longer a slave, but God's child" (Galatians 4:7); "I am seen as precious" (Isaiah 43:4); and "I am God's special possession." (1 Peter 2:9)

Father God, help me to see who You made me to be, and empower me to stay true to my identity In Christ. Amen.

Go Boldly!

Jessica Wilson

So let us come boldly to the throne of our gracious God. There we will receive his mercy, and we will find grace to help us when we need it most.
Hebrews 4:16 (NLT)

If you had asked me to describe my prayer life just a few months ago, I probably would have said, "safe, complacent, self-centered."

In a quiet moment while praying over my son, God spoke and told me to go boldly before Him and in that moment, my prayer life changed.

I started studying the book of Nehemiah and came to understand that he was a man who had a heart for God and the things that were special to Him.

He understood and believed that God is merciful. His belief was rooted in the Word of God which encouraged him often to seek the Lord.

He understood that prayer was all about God.

When our hearts are synched with His, we will see God work in our lives. He invites us to do life with Him. We can approach

Him because He supremely reigns over everything and as children of God, He has given us stewardship over the earth.

When we connect with God through prayer, it's a personal connection that transforms and fuels us. We experience fullness of life when we have relationship with Him and include Him in our lives.

He invites us to go boldly before Him. We are not meant to do life alone, rather to depend on Him. God will remember His promises which never waiver.

Loving Father, thank You that You are near, that You are with me and that I am not alone. I come boldly before You. I speak the promises that You have spoken over my life and trust that those promises will be fulfilled. In Jesus' name, amen.

I Love Grackles!

Julia Lutz

This is the confidence we have in approaching God: That if we ask anything according to his will, he hears us.
1 John 5:14 (NIV)

I hate bird poop. Don't you?

The Grackle is a large, long legged, long billed blackbird native to North and South America. It makes a variety of sounds like a croak, high pitched whistle or squeak. Males more than females seem to communicate with me. I don't understand why they pick me!

For some unknown reason, of all the trees in my yard, they have chosen, by the hundreds, to nest in my old live oak tree just outside the back door. Morning till dusk they "bird talk," even in the quiet, peaceful night. I will hear an arousing squeak, or sometimes they act like night guards conversing with one another. Regardless, they keep me up!

Every day, I take my broom and go outside to wash the bird poop off the porch. One day, I had this conversation with God:

"God, I know you can talk to those Grackles like you talk to me! Tell them to poop on the grass or somewhere else, but not my porch." (Pretty stupid for me to tell God what to do, right?)

"I could kill them."

Then God spoke, "I made the Grackles. They are mine."

"But in my tree, God?"

"I made the tree and the water in the hose. And I gave you the money for the water," God said.

"Sorry, God, I'll shut up."

Suddenly, I thought, "What if I didn't have the money? Or the water? No tree, no home and no birds? What if I didn't hear from God? What if there was no Jesus?"

Interesting thing, the other day while pulling weeds, the Grackles warned me of a snake in my flower bed. Now I really love Grackles!

Thank You, Lord, for teaching me a simple lesson on how to appreciate the sounds, the birds and all the blessings you give me daily. I love you. In Jesus' name, amen.

Good Plans

Kelly Mays

For I know the plans I have for you, says the Lord. They are plans for good and not for disaster to give you a future and a hope. Jeremiah 29:11 (NLT)

Those words bring me to tears. My life verse…my mantra. My reason to keep hanging on, even when everything seems lost. I have clung to them through good times, hard times and seemingly impossible times. God in all His gracious mercy illuminated this verse for me shortly before the hardest years of my life.

It was during a ladies' Bible study, when I let these words sink deep into my heart, when I truly read them and drank in their depth for the first time. God's great love for me became so apparent, almost tangible.

During the study, I was asked what my favorite part of this lesson was. As tears rolled down my cheeks, I recited this verse. You see, like so many, my life up to this point had been hard. Bad decisions, sin, and a life of disobedience to God. But then there had been the hard circumstances at the hands of others. The ones beyond my control. The ones that left wounds and scars that no one could see.

I had such a hard time wrapping my mind around someone not wanting to harm me. But God's word says, "God is not a man, so he does not lie" (Numbers 23:19). So, if I believe this verse, I must believe Jeremiah 29:11.

That was the turning point. Imagine, He has good plans to give us all hope and a future. I cling to those words of hope when my life is upside down. To trust Him in all his sovereignty, when nothing else makes sense, and I am on my face crying out in prayer. Sometimes, while driving down the road in my car, I scream out this mantra at the top of my lungs to God, to myself and to the enemy.

Abba Father, thank You for your Word that sees us through the good times, the hard times and the seemingly impossible times. Give my sisters a Word that will provide direction to their lives, and a Word to which they can cling. Amen.

Death, Where Is Your Sting?

Linda Serrano

Precious in the sight of the Lord is the death of his saints.
Psalm 116:15 (KJV)

As I sat in my mother's hospital room watching the nurse administer the procedure that had become so familiar to us over the past several months, I struggled with the fact that her condition was deteriorating.

My mother Nellie was a godly woman who had a meek spirit and a kind heart. She had been diagnosed with cancer a year and half earlier and had chosen not to undergo conventional treatment.

Although she had said she "wanted to go home," there was an army of Christians, friends and family members praying on her behalf with steadfast faith.

I was my mother's primary caregiver and had a close-up view of how much she was suffering.

While she was being treated that day, I decided to escape to the chapel to talk with the Lord and seek guidance. I asked Him to speak to me concerning my mom, knowing that we are all here for a season and that our lives are in His hands.

After I prayed, I walked over to the altar where there was a big Bible. I asked the Lord to speak to me through His Word and, as I opened the Bible, my eyes fell on the Scripture, *"Precious in the sight of the Lord is the death of his saints."*

Through my tears, I thanked God for His sweet, straightforward response.

This beautiful Scripture is engraved on my mom's tombstone.

Dear Lord, thank You for your Word that speaks truth to us in every situation. In Jesus' name, amen.

The Promise Of Peace

Lucie Grove

Surely He has borne our griefs and carried our sorrows...
Isaiah 53:4 (NKJV)

In 1985, my beloved husband Dan, the pastor of the Mooringsport Methodist Church in Louisiana, was diagnosed with a rare neurological disease which caused him to have to resign from the wonderful church. He later passed away.

After we lost Dan, things went along smoothly for several years then tragedy struck again. Both of my precious sons – Danny and John – died in separate highway accidents.

Through the years, I found this verse to be true and it has comforted me through the most difficult times in my life.

I really missed Dan. We had spent twenty years in the United States Air Force where he was a lieutenant colonel and we enjoyed twelve years in the excitement of the Charismatic Renewal. And we had two wonderful sons and a daughter.

With Dan gone, I had questions: Could I keep two of my children in college? Should I go back to nursing?

And I knew I would really miss the wonderful Mooringsport

church family. Thankfully, God showed himself faithful and provided for all of our needs.

During those difficult times, my heart was encouraged and comforted by this particular verse. I also learned to lean on the passage of Scripture in Philippians 4, which says, "…and the peace of God, which surpasses all understanding, will guard your hearts and minds through Christ Jesus."

I chose to stand on this promise and it became my constant companion as I repeated it over and over every day. Although I lost my husband and sons, I realized through the Scriptures that going to heaven is not a disaster but a great victory.

By standing on God's promises of peace and victory, He always proved faithful.

Thank You, Lord, for your wonderful peace that gives us strength to have victory even in the most difficult times. In Jesus' name, amen.

My New Faith

Maimuna Mbeh

You are the light of the world. A town built on a hill cannot be hidden.
Neither do people light a lamp and put it under a bowl. Instead they put it
on its stand, and it gives light to everyone in the house. In the same way, let
your light shine before others, that they may see your good deeds and glorify
your Father in heaven.
Matthew 5:14 (NIV)

I grew up in a strict Muslim home in Nigeria but was always fascinated with Christianity. I admired its traditions and freedom to practice faith. I loved the songs that I learned to sing but did not know what they meant.

After I married my husband Abel and had two children, I met Hassana. She also came from a Muslim culture and converted to Christianity under her father's roof. I learned that her conversion brought severe persecution from her parents, her siblings and the entire Muslim community. But she held on to her faith.

Watching the Holy Spirit completely transform Hassana's life and her relationships with others compelled me to the source of her change. Her undisclosed strength was Jesus. She encouraged me to accept Him as my Lord and personal Savior. She gave me a Bible, which led me to embrace Jesus and leave my Muslim faith.

For three months, I hid my faith from my family. I feared telling my father who was an Imam (a religious leader in the Muslim faith). I was afraid of what he would do to me when he found that I had converted. His reputation and position were so dear to him, killing any of his children who would convert to another religion would come easy to him.

In the meantime, my faith in Christ grew by reading the Word and the Holy Spirit filled my soul with boldness which conquered my fears.

In time, I told my parents and though I experienced many trials and tribulations, the Lord was with me. And I am here to share my story.

This verse helped me to understand that I am called to be a light in the world. I was created to shine. I want to be a living testimony of how I conquered the fears of the past and how He gave me boldness to share His love with others.

Thank You, Father, that You never failed me and You never abandoned me.
So, I can say in confidence, "You are my helper and I will have no fear."
Amen.

Keys To Freedom

Mary Mendez

…For the weapons of our warfare are not carnal, but mighty through God to the pulling down of strong holds; Casting down imaginations, and every high thing that exalteth itself against the knowledge of God, and bringing into captivity every thought to the obedience of Christ…
2 Corinthians 10:4-7 (KJV)

As a Christian for many years, one of the greatest truths I have learned is how to defeat spiritual strongholds in our lives. The battlefield begins in the mind and we must guard ourselves to keep from being in agreement with the father of lies. So, how do we tear down or dismantle a stronghold which is a lie of the enemy?

Based on my experience, I want to share with you the keys to the pulling down strongholds.

First key: If the enemy has any legal right for the stronghold in your life, ask the Holy Spirit to reveal it to you. Once you identify it, ask Him to reveal the truth which He promises in His Word to do.

Second key: Repent for believing the lie and remember Satan doesn't play fair.

Third key: Forgive yourself for believing the lie and/or forgive anyone who may have caused you to believe the lie. You can renounce it and break its power because of the finished work of Jesus Christ at the cross.

Fourth key: Declare the truth which is found in the Word of God. Example: "God has loved me with an everlasting love; therefore, He has drawn me with 'loving devotion" (Jeremiah 31:3)," or "...for he who touches me, touches the apple of His eye..." (Zechariah 2:8) instead of saying "no one loves me."

Fifth key: Allow God, the Holy Spirit, and Jesus to reveal what is inside your mind, your will or your emotions and begin to pull down that stronghold and cast out that imagination.

Remember that God is your Protector. He loves you. He is the Lion of Judah, the Great I Am, the Creator of the universe and He does not want you entangled and enslaved by the strongholds of the enemy.

Thank You, Lord, for setting me free from spiritual strongholds by believing and declaring the truth of your Word. In Jesus' name, amen.

Abiding

Maye Moore

If ye abide in me, and my words abide in you, ye shall ask what ye will, and it shall be done unto you.
John 15:7 (KJV)

Meditation on the Word of God can be exciting and revealing. Sometimes God really captures your attention. While meditating on this verse, the Holy Spirit began to teach me this promise: if I abide in Him – that is to remain in Him – then He remains in me. Thus, in order to abide in Him, it requires action on my part. I am to remain in His presence.

As we come into the presence of the Most High God, our communion with Him becomes a source of strength and renewal. Then we have fellowship with Him through prayer and reading His Word.

John 15:5 says that Jesus is the vine and we are His branches; if we remain in Him and He in us, we will bear much fruit. We are connected to the vine. When we plant God's Word in our hearts, the seed(s) begin to grow and produce much fruit.

Soon we will have a harvest for the Kingdom of God. We are

like a tree planted by the river that brings forth its fruit in due season. What we sow, we reap.

When we plant an apple seed in the ground, that seed will produce fruit after its own kind. Just think of all the seeds found in one apple tree. And it only took one seed to produce a harvest.

Not only understanding the seed of the Word, but praying it completely changed my life. As a result, the supernatural began to manifest. It produced miracles and brought life, health and wholeness. Surely, Jesus is our Provision!

Precious women of God, we must guard our hearts and not allow the devil steal our time. Let us plant the seeds to create a harvest as we abide (remain) continually in Jesus and His Word.

Lord Jesus, I desire to bear fruit that will remain and glorify your Name. Give me wisdom, knowledge and understanding as I abide in your Word. In Jesus' name, amen.

A Wonderful Counselor

Natalia Meltabarger

For a child is born to us, a son is given to us. The government will rest on his shoulders. And He will be called: Wonderful Counselor, Mighty God, Everlasting Father, Prince of Peace. Isaiah 9:6 (NLT)

On a crisp fall day in November, I was reading Isaiah 9 when this particular verse inspired me. It is a favorite Scripture for the Christmas season and, in fact, it is likely that you have read it before.

A specific portion of this verse caught my eye: "He will be called, Wonderful Counselor." I could not help but pause and consider everything this phrase meant to me. Such an amazing thought! Before any of us realized we would even need a Wonderful Counselor, God went to great lengths to make preparations for us.

So, when confusion beckons to pull us away, let us lean on our Counselor for He is good and kind during our most difficult circumstances. He is our mighty God who makes provision for us even before we need it.

Our everlasting Father bottles up our tears, reminding us we are precious in His sight. He is familiar with suffering and is our greatest intercessor. He does not turn away from our pain.

His Holy Spirit helps and teaches us as we are faithful to pray and read His Word. There is no greater love than His. We can trust the promises of God and hope and peace are found in Him.

Father God, what a precious thought to know that You are the wonderful Counselor. Thank You for making provision for us even before we recognize our need. And we will continue to praise You forevermore. Amen.

God Has No Pets

Pat Lewis

Trust in the Lord with all your heart and lean not to your own understanding. In all your ways acknowledge Him and He will direct your path.
Proverbs 3:5-6 (KJV)

Recently, one of my bright granddaughters lost her job. She was devastated! A recent college graduate, she was thrilled to be employed in the corporate world and had received a promotion to the human resources division.

The company had a very bad quarter and restructuring and downsizing was underway. She was the low man on the totem pole; last hired, first to go!

My grandchildren often call me for prayer when there is a problem in their lives. I usually sympathize and pray for divine intervention, but not this time! The Lord immediately brought this particular Scripture to mind. I counseled her that losing her job was not a disaster but a course-correction for her.

I know that God has a special purpose and plan for my granddaughter, as He does for all of us. I also know that He loves her enough to intervene.

My role was to encourage her to keep acknowledging God as Savior and Guide. I knew from experience that He would direct her path. Shortly thereafter, the Lord opened a door for a breakfast interview with a company owned by believers.

In less than two weeks, we observed a dramatic illustration of the truth in God's Word.

Beloved, God has no pets. He loves us all the same. We need to know His Word and stand on it. He waits for us to call on Him. He wants us to succeed! "If God be for us who can be against us" (Romans. 8:31).

The condition to the promise is to acknowledge Him in all our ways. This means trying to please Him in all that we do, forsaking the pull of the world and standing with Him, according to His Word.

Heavenly Father, we hold before your throne this day not only ourselves, but all our offspring. We understand that You love them more than we do. We ask that You keep adjusting the course of their lives to conform with your purpose. Shine a bright light on their paths as they realize your truth and reality. We hold to your promise to save the seed of the righteous. In Jesus' name, amen.

Nothing Is Impossible

Patricia Binkley-Childress

If we are faithless, He remains faithful,
for He cannot deny Himself.
2 Timothy 2:13 (NASB)

As I was rereading the story of Sarai, Abram, and God's promise for an heir in Genesis 18, I was reminded of why their son was given the name Isaac which means "he laughs."

Of course, if God told me I was going to have a child at ninety-nine years old, I think I would laugh, too. But when we know God's promises yet we go through life worrying or thinking the worst about a situation we are facing, we are really laughing at God!

The Bible is filled with many examples of situations that seemed impossible: Noah built a huge Ark, basically by himself, while people laughed at him and told him he was crazy.

Many, many small armies faced large armies yet won. Daniel faced lions and lived. David faced Goliath and killed him!

Shadrach, Meshach and Abednego not only lived through the fiery furnace; they came out not even smelling like smoke. They faced the impossible yet were unharmed because they had faith that God would deliver them and He did!

What can we do when we lose our jobs and cannot pay bills or buy food? When we are told by doctors that we have a disease with a poor prognosis? When our house burns down or is blown away by a storm and all our earthly possessions are gone?

Or what about when all our dreams and what we have worked to achieve is destroyed by closed doors? We are laughing at God and His promise to work all things out for our good and His glory, when our response to what seems impossible is anxiety, doubt or fear!

George Mueller once said: «Faith does not operate in the realm of the possible. There is no glory for God in that which is humanly possible. Faith begins where man›s power ends.»

It is at those impossible times we must remember, *"If we are faithless, HE REMAINS FAITHFUL."*

Father in Heaven, I pray that no matter how dark, how dreary, or how impossible the situation I may be faced with today that I will rest in your faithfulness and in knowing that with You all things are possible! Amen.

All Things

Rachel Wilson

And we know that all things work together for the good of those who love God, who are called according to his purpose... Romans 8:28 (NET)

This life is filled with both big and small challenges. As wives, mothers, or simply as humans, we are burdened constantly by the myriad things we have to do day to day.

Many women have shared with me that they feel like they are always in the middle of a very complicated juggling act and I agree. There are times when I find myself overwhelmed because something that I labored on relentlessly did not turn out the way I thought it should.

It might be at home, with my husband, with my kids or something personal. But I have always been encouraged by the fact that this verse uses the word "all" when speaking about those things that are worked together for our good by the Father. There isn't anything that He leaves out.

As a believer, I have held onto this verse as a promise from God. Every success and challenge, every joy and heartbreak, even the losses and setbacks in our lives are used by the Lord to bless us.

When we are tempted to be angry at God or others around us because of our circumstances, we have to know the truth that each event of our lives is known to the Father.

He sees us, He calls us and He is right there with us as we go through life. If we are to be witnesses to others in our circle of influence, then we have to truly believe that every bad event in our lives is actually something that will be used to glorify Him.

Father, help me to trust You every day with the events of my life. I believe that You are working all things together to bless me. In Jesus' name, amen.

Be Good, Do Good, That's Real Good!

Rebecca Cleere

*Keep your behavior excellent among the Gentiles, so that in the thing in
which they slander you as evildoers,
they may because of your good deeds, as they observe them, glorify God in the
day of visitation.
1 Peter 2:12 (NAS)*

When I was growing up, I remember being told to be good
and do good. Today, I teach this principle to my students at church.
There is a reason that we MUST behave in a certain manner.

God has called us to be *different* from the world. The way that
non-believers see us talking/acting/treating others will directly
affect the way they respond to the God we serve.

This passage encourages and reminds me that I am called to be
good for a purpose. Many people say nice things and have excellent
behavior but if it's not for the right reason, it is ultimately in vain.

There have been times and situations in my life when someone
has complimented me by a response or behavior. It would be easy
to just say "thank you" and move along, but I cannot take the
credit. My natural inclination is to be selfish and think about how

I will be affected.

Jesus showed us the correct way to treat all people and that is what I strive to do when someone compliments me. The credit goes where it is due and that's to Jesus.

I have heard it said that people will forget what they say but will remember the way you make them feel. Our words and actions have power and we need to use it to lead others to the Lord. My mantra and mission in life is to love God and people.

Lord, help me to act according to your Word. I want to see people and situations the way You do. I want to love them the way that You do. Help me to accomplish this today and every day. Amen.

Freedom From Fear

Rebecca Joy Hardin

I sought the Lord, and He heard me,
and delivered me from all my fears.
Psalm 34:4 (KJV)

There's one way to have freedom from fear and that is to seek the Lord. When we seek Him, He answers and delivers us from all of our fears. In our household, we look to Him to deliver us from "all, all, all" fears.

No matter the source of your fear – a troubled child, an illness, a financial need, your marriage – Psalm 34 covers them all.

The beginning of this Psalm encourages us to bless the Lord at all times; His praises should always be on our lips; and to magnify and boast in Him.

Always remember, the Lord inhabits the praises of His people. As we praise Him, His presence covers us and there is joy forevermore. His joy is our strength. Where the spirit of the Lord is, there is liberty. Fear cannot "hang around" in His presence.

During his time of fear, King David cried to the Lord and He heard him and saved him out of all his troubles. David knew that

God would protect and rescue him. As a matter of fact, he could taste and see that the Lord was good. How blessed are we when we take refuge in Him because we will not lack any good thing.

No matter what situation we face, our Savior waits for us to seek Him, cry out to Him and receive His tender mercies. The battle belongs to the Lord! And we can be encouraged by Isaiah 41:10 to not fear for He is with us; do not be dismayed for He is our God.

Heavenly Father, thank You for capturing our hearts with your perfect love. Thank You for setting us free as we release all of our fears to You and for answering us in miraculous ways for your glory. Amen.

Peace Of Mind

Rhonda Baker

I will both lie down in peace, and sleep;
For You alone, O Lord, make me dwell in safety.
Psalm 4:8 (NKJV)

Sleepless nights are not unfamiliar to most of us. They come for a variety of reasons. New parents getting up when their baby awakes, and then they try to fall asleep again. Your people are out of town and you are at home alone. Worries about a relationship. Concerns for our family. Stress about work. Anxiety about finances. Issues with our health.

For some, these nights are few and far between. For others, they come more often. Our minds simply will not shut down. A million "what ifs" run through our minds:

What if he says this? What if my kids get hurt? What if this presentation does not go well? What if I can't forgive them? What if they can't forgive me? What if the money doesn't come through? What if she doesn't want to be my friend? What if this is going too well?

While some of the concerns and "what ifs" may be justified,

our minds often take them to a whole new level. I heard well-known author Beth Moore call them "vain imaginations and spewing minds." These "what ifs" scenarios play out to the fullest and then escalate each time they are replayed.

When I have my own anxious nights and my mind tries to wind down, this Psalm has become solid ground for me. I have quoted it to myself before my head even hits the pillow. I have repeated it over and over on my bed while clutching my Bible.

The truth is I can lie down in peace and sleep because God is with me. In every "what if" that comes to fruition and all those that don't, Jesus Christ is with me. He will not leave me nor forsake me. In the good and the bad, His Holy Spirit is dwelling within me, guiding me if I will listen. God, alone, makes me dwell in safety.

Sisters in Christ, He will do the same for you.

Jesus, Thank You for your Word which reminds us where our peace comes from. We are grateful You know the frailty of our minds and how easily we can be caught up in anxious thoughts. Help us to remember we can put our heads down at night and sleep, for we are held by You. Amen.

Don't Waste His Blood

Sharon Shelton

*Therefore, (there is) now no condemnation (no adjudging guilty of wrong)
for those who are in Christ Jesus.
Romans 8:1 (AMP)*

This text is simple, yet its meaning is profound! Most all Christians are very familiar with this verse and can recite it by heart. And THAT can be a problem: over-familiarity. Thus, we miss the depth of its meaning.

The Lord tells us here that when we miss the mark such as fighting with our husbands, snapping at our children, feeling sorry for ourselves, shouting a nickname under our breath to bully drivers, later we may find ourselves full of remorse. Real regret. Even to the point of self-loathing. We may even condemn ourselves for falling into the same sin trap over and over.

But God does not condemn us. He knows what sin still lurks in our flesh. He sent His Son as an offering and condemned our sin in the flesh and deprived its power over all who accept that sacrifice, according to Romans 8:3.

This sin in the flesh is what the Apostle Paul grappled with in Romans Chapter 7. Notice that the Word does not tell us that sin in the flesh has been obliterated. That's why we still find ourselves missing the mark after accepting Jesus Christ as our Savior.

So be done with self-condemnation! Let's not waste another drop of Jesus' blood for past, present or future sins for that matter. Let's decide today to stop condemning ourselves and let Jesus' beaten flesh and spilled blood do its work on our behalf. Hence, we deprive that sin of its power to bring death through condemnation.

Once we stop condemning ourselves, we become less critical and judgmental toward others. Because: "Condemned people condemn people."

Wonderful Father, thank You for delivering us from the power of sin's condemnation. Thank You for acquitting us and granting us the gift of righteousness instead. May all praise and glory and honor be to our Lord Jesus! Amen.

Us To Him, Him To Us

Sherry Bridwell

...and when He gave thanks, He broke it and said, "This is my body, which is for you; do this in remembrance of Me." In the same way He took the cup also after supper, saying, "This cup is the covenant in My blood; do this as often as you drink it, in remembrance of Me...
1 Corinthians 11:23-26 (NAS)

When I take communion at church, these Scriptures always speak to me. One day the Holy Spirit prompted me to dig deeper into the true meaning of this word. I learned that "commune" means to share or an exchange of intimate thoughts and feelings especially on a mental or spiritual level and that is what happens when we take communion.

We were redeemed and made righteous because of Jesus' sacrifice on the cross. It is our relationship with Him that makes communion so meaningful on a deeper level of what truly is our inheritance that took place at Calvary that day.

Not only do we commune with Him, but He expresses His feelings and thoughts with us.

The first time I experienced this deep intimacy with Him was in a Bible study. We had a lesson on this subject matter and as one of the ladies passed the elements, I suddenly saw Jesus with the elements in His hands passing them out and He turned to me and said, "I did this for you."

From that day forward, communion became very personal to me. I would encourage you to open your heart and allow Him to connect with you because this precious time with Him is a two-way exchange: us to Him and Him to us.

Father in Heaven, thank You for your body and blood that was sacrificed so I could be made whole. You are the author of my faith. Strengthen me to realize all You paid for me. Your Word says that the sheep hear the Shepherd's voice and I want to hear your voice. In Jesus' name, amen.

Jealousy

Sloane Keith

A heart at peace gives life to the body, but envy rots the bones. Proverbs 14:30 (NIV)

Do you ever compare yourself with other women while scrolling through social media, at the grocery store, or coffee shop and wish you had what they had? Maybe it's their physical traits, success or how perfect their lives appear at first glance.

I want you to know, Sis, that you are not alone in this common hold the enemy has on many women. It is called jealousy and it is when women fall into a constant trap of comparison by speaking words contrary to what God says and thinks about you.

I have learned and experienced in my own life and have seen in the lives of other Christian women how the enemy traps us into believing these lies. As a result, it creates a feeling of envy towards others which ultimately affects the condition of our hearts.

It doesn't change the person or situation when I envy but it affects me when I no longer have peace in my heart. I begin to believe things that are far from true and are not what God says about me.

So, my challenge to you is to ask yourself immediately the next time you begin to envy: "Is this what God says and thinks about me?" If the answer is no, then you know it's a lie and do not believe it.

Fight envy with encouragement and, as promised in this verse, you will experience a heart at peace giving life to your body.

Dear Lord, help me to be confident in who You created me to be and not fall into the trap of jealousy and comparison. Help me to speak life over myself and others whenever those feelings come over me.

In Jesus' name, amen.

Balancing The Scales

Tabitha May-DeBoer

A false balance is an abomination to the LORD, but a just weight is His delight.
Proverbs 11:1 (KJV)

This verse intrigues me because it has been used over and over, pointing out God's disgust with dishonesty.

Nothing is more offensive to God than a false balance. But there is more to this verse. Balance is essential for an abundance of tangible things like scales, tables, tires, hormones and homes. Imagine living in a home that is not level.

What about the unseen things in your life, like your heart, your work, your energy or your time?

On a scale of one to ten, how would you rate your balance between home and work? How about your personal or professional relationships?

When balance is lost, it creates chaos when neglected for a prolonged period of time. Marriages fail, money becomes unmanageable and friends disappoint you.

What about your relationship with yourself? Do you need

balance? Yes, we all need balance to keep us healthy and happy.

God does not want us to struggle to achieve goals or dreams or to neglect valuable things. God wants us to have a *shalom* life that is whole and complete. Balance is stable and appraises the value of one thing to another.

Today, make a list of the top five things that are valuable to you. Then, weigh the time you spend on each. Does your balance of energy, money and time reflect what you really value?

Lord, help me balance what is valuable. Guide my heart and hands to invest in the important things You have placed in my life. Give me wisdom to manage my time, energy and money. Do not let me have a false balance that does not reflect your heart and my destiny. In Jesus' name, amen.

Have I Searched My Heart?

Tara Keith Hickman

"But a person must [prayerfully] examine himself [and his relationship to Christ], and only when he has done so should he eat of the bread and drink of the cup."
1 Corinthians 11:28 (AMP)

We ALL know the drill…the preacher reads the passage of Scripture; ushers pass out trays with crackers and juice. We hold the elements as he encourages each of us to examine our hearts. Then there's music, a short prayer, then we partake. DONE…until next quarter.

Can we possibly believe that our familiarity with the verses, our half-hearted prayers and rote participation in this ritual have any effect? Have our hearts become so calloused and holiness so routine, that we don't even know how to answer the simple questions, "Have I searched my heart?" And then BOOM… "Will I be OBEDIENT?"

The Holy Scriptures are crystal clear that we are to carefully and prayerfully examine our hearts before observing the Lord's Supper. To do so in a careless manner denies the finished work of

Jesus on the Cross.

So, during those few moments of silence, ask the Holy Spirit to show you: Do you need to deal with sin in your life? Do you have relationships that need healing? Are there areas where there are strongholds of fear? And the list goes on...

One Sunday morning, our pastor was reading this passage and I was suddenly struck with the realization that I had been carrying resentment, anger and unforgiveness in my heart for more than a year.

It was the first time in my Christian walk of forty-five years that I KNEW I could not take Communion. I was devastated. But over the next few months or so, as the Holy Spirit gently convicted me, I obediently dealt with my sin, repented, sought counsel, forgave and was reconciled to several dear people, including family members. As of this writing, my conscience is clear...FREEDOM!

Holy Father, as I come to your table, may I do so in a reverent manner, remembering Jesus and His sacrifice for me on the cross. Expose sin in my life. May I be quick to forgive as You have so freely forgiven me. Father, I praise and thank You for the privilege of enjoying your table and walking in Your freedom! Amen.

I Am Always With You

Vivian Fernand Narcisse

What's more, I am with you,
and I will protect you wherever you go.
Genesis 28:15 (NLT)

Have you ever done anything so outrageous and out of character as to move 2000 miles away from home? Well, I did!

In 2000, I came to the United States from Suriname, South America, to a new culture and unfamiliar environment where I had no loved ones or friends. I recall the first few months were challenging which caused me to draw closer to the Lord and to know Him in an extraordinarily, unique and personal way.

There were times when my faith was tested but strengthened. God not only provided ALL my needs, but He blessed me with an amazing, loving spiritual church family in Baton Rouge, Louisiana.

Twelve years later, God planted my feet in Longview, Texas, and, once again, He proved Himself faithful. He met my needs including a new spiritual family and blessed me with my husband.

Today, we live on the East Coast. With this recent move, God made it clear to me that relationships are not only necessary but a blessing from Him. He pours out His love and faithfulness upon us through the people He brings into our lives.

Through these transitions, I have learned that everything we have (family, friends, work, material possessions and finances) is a gift from God. Most importantly, He also wants us to know Him intimately as our Provider and Protector.

Furthermore, God amazingly taught me that He is the source of my life, and that my circumstances do not limit Him. That is why we should look to Him for everything.

God, thank You for your presence and that you are with me wherever I go.
Thank You for your promise that You will never leave me nor forsake me and
will provide, guide, strengthen and protect me in every season of my life.
Today, I choose to trust in You no matter my circumstances.
In Jesus' name, amen.

Look Up!

Vivian Bustillos Keith

*Now when things begin to happen, look up and lift up your heads, because
your redemption draws near.*
Luke 21:28 (NKJV)

Life can bring many challenges or storms, as I call them. And
when they suddenly appear, I tend to think about Jesus in the
boat with the disciples during a severe storm. Sweet Jesus was fast
asleep while the disciples were frantic and fearing for their lives.
When they called out to him, He got up, rebuked the wind and
said, "Peace be still" (Matthew 37:41).

Not too long ago, I had one of those moments filled with
stress, anxiety, discouragement and sadness all wrapped up in one
with a note from the enemy saying, "Have a nice day."

I was so distraught that I did not have the spiritual strength
to quote any Scripture for encouragement, or even think about
Jesus calming the storm. Instead, I let my emotions take over. God
saw what I was going through and He knew that I needed to be
encouraged.

What I heard next was my cell phone. To my surprise it was

from Mary Jo, a dear friend whom I had not heard from in a good while.

Our relationship goes back to when we were young single moms at Calvary Temple in Irving, Texas, and I was happy to hear from her. As we talked, I could not help but share my heart and what was going on in my life.

Mary Jo listened and she said something to me that was so simple and yet so profound. She said, "Vivian, look up! When you don't know what to do, just look up!"

At that moment, I felt like God was speaking to me through my friend and a sense of relief and a burden was lifted off of me.

There will be times in your lives when calamity, a financial hardship or emotional pain may come knocking on your door. In this verse of Scripture, Jesus tells us to look up, our redemption draws near. That, my beloved, is good news!

God is aware of your every situation and He cares. He will redeem you. Allow Him to move on your behalf. It may not be what you expect…but you see, He can move in mysterious ways and He knows what you need. Just like He used Mary Jo, my friend, to reach out to me in my time of need, He will do the same for you!

Lord, You are my Redeemer and You intervene during my time of need.
Thank You for never leaving me nor forsaking me.
All glory and honor to You. Amen.

Deeper

Alaina Strait

When you go through deep waters, I will be with you...
Isaiah 43:2 (NLT)

Nothing brings me happier memories than those times swimming with my family.

I am a mother of two awesome kids, Jackson and Cara. And when it comes to our summers, we love spending time in the pool. My kids jump in regardless of the temperature.

If you are like me, you stand in one place allowing your body to acclimate. It's slow and steady. Stepping into the shallow water allows my body to adjust to the temperature. As I wade in the water, I can decide to stand there, float for a while, go underwater or swim into the deep.

Question: Where are you in this picture? Do you wade into the shallow or like my kids, do you skip all that and plunge into the deep?

From a spiritual standpoint going deeper with God is different for everyone. Neither approach is wrong; however, I think that if we plunge into the deep, we can miss the benefits of wading in the shallow water.

Wading and working toward the deep water allows us to draw close to God in a more intimate manner. Through this experience, we can see who He is and what He wants to do in our lives. In time, you will find yourself swimming in the deep, trusting and relying on God and developing an amazing relationship with Him.

Want to go deeper with God? Here's how: Develop a consistent prayer life and stay in the Word of God. Be willing to say yes and do what God is asking you to do. Be courageous and take the challenge to go deeper with Him. And be excited to take this journey!

Thank You, Lord, for calling us to go deeper with You. Thank You for being patient and tenderly leading us. We love and trust You with every area of our lives. Amen.

Humility

Allison Wolfe Cunningham

*Humble yourselves, therefore, under God's mighty hand, that he may lift you
up in due time. Cast all your anxiety on him because he cares for you.*
1 Peter 5:6-7 (NIV)

When children are little, they are fearless. They implicitly trust
the adults in their lives. Toddlers love to be thrown up in the air
and caught. At a swimming pool you will see their exuberant faces
as they anticipate jumping into the deep end knowing they will be
swooped up before going under.

My kids always loved to walk around our house standing on
my husband's feet. The closeness to their Daddy and thrill of going
wherever he is taking them is exhilarating.

As adults, we lose this sense of security. However, the Lord
desires our trust in Him to be this fearless! It pleases His heart
when we willingly place ourselves into the hands of our Savior
knowing He holds our hearts and lives secure.

We have to make a choice. Pride or humility. Pride is rooted in
fear and insecurity which requires self-reliance and control. This
produces anxiety because the pressures, disappointments and trials

of life are too heavy to bear. In an effort to handle life on our own, we resort to destructive behaviors which lead us to bondage.

God is a gracious and loving Father who instructs us through the Scriptures to choose a better way: humility. It comes from security in Christ; knowing we belong to Jesus and, like little children, His grace catches us in the deep waters of life.

It is an act of our will to recognize and position ourselves into the care of hands that are mightier than our own. It pleases the Father when we give the cares and worries over to Him. This act of faith requires us to relinquish our understanding and trust in God's providential work in our lives.

However, it always works in our favor. There is a divine exchange: love instead of fear. Peace for worry. Hope drives out depression. Choosing humility opens the door for intimacy with Christ. His faithfulness and unfailing love come into full view which leads us to freedom.

Jesus, forgive me of my pride and lead me to humble pathways.
Thank You for being steadfast and true. Amen.

The Enemy's Strategy: Deception

Andrée Elliott

*But if you [men representing King Hezekiah of Judah], say to me
[Rabshakeh from the King of Assyria], 'We trust in the LORD our God.
Is not He, Whose high places and Whose altars Hezekiah has taken away,
and has said to Judah and Jerusalem, You will worship before this altar in
Jerusalem?*
2 Kings 18:22 (ONMB)

Sennacherib, king of Assyria, had taken all the fortified cities of Judah and was threatening to take Jerusalem. He also sent men to intimidate King Hezekiah and the people within the walls of Jerusalem.

Notice the strategy of Judah's enemy: the speaking of mocking and intimidating words – deceptive words that expressed twisted truth meant to instill fear and doubt that God would save them. Yes, King Hezekiah did remove altars in high places, but what were these high places?

According to 2 Kings 18:4, Hezekiah broke images and cut down groves and broke in pieces the brazen serpent that Moses made and that the children of Israel worshipped! These high places were places of idolatry. So, is this enemy's strategy reminiscent of any other deception in the Bible?

The Garden of Eden? Yes! In the same way that the enemy (the serpent) spoke to Eve, he spoke to Hezekiah and the people of Judah. And he still speaks to us today; his strategy has not changed: Satan still twists truth, mocks, and intimidates in an attempt to get us to fear and doubt God.

How should we respond? We can learn a lesson from the people of Judah and King Hezekiah: they did not answer the enemy a word, and Hezekiah humbled himself and prayed. The result? The LORD miraculously delivered Judah from the Assyrians.

In the same way, we ought not entertain thoughts that instill fear and cause us to doubt God. And we should humble ourselves and pray to the LORD for help whenever the enemy mocks and intimidates. The LORD hears. He answers. And He delivers us!

Father, help me to study your Word so that I recognize twisted truth. Prompt me to humble myself and pray. And thank You, LORD, that You always hear and answer to help me in every situation. Amen.

The Joshua And Caleb Spirit

Beth Collins

Then Caleb quieted the people before Moses, and said,
"Let us go up at once and take possession of it;
for we will certainly conquer it."
Numbers. 13:30 (AMP)

Because of unbelief, rebellion and complaining, the first generation of Israelites were not allowed to go into their promised land and died from a plague in the wilderness. However, God gave the Promised Land to the second generation.

What generation are you going to be a part of? I don't know about you, but I want to be a part of the generation that receives everything God has for them.

Moses chose twelve spies to go into the Promised Land to see what enemies they were up against. When they returned, Joshua and Caleb brought a positive report and said that they should conquer and take possession of the land. But the other ten spies complained about the giants. They said that compared to the giants, the spies looked like grasshoppers!

What was the difference in these spies? Joshua and Caleb

chose to step out and dared to believe that God was with them. The other ten did not trust God, rather yielded to fear of the giants in the land.

Whether you are facing a giant of depression, a chronic illness, a child with a disability, or a broken marriage, God is able to bring victory in your life.

I believe we can learn a valuable truth from this Scripture. The first step to conquer the challenges in our lives is to quiet the voices. "Caleb quieted the people" from complaining and he chose to come in agreement with what God said.

Ask the Holy Spirit today to speak words of truth about your situation and reject the lies of the enemy.

Father God, reveal truth about what You have for me in my Promised Land. I repent for coming into agreement with the lies of the enemy. Amen.

Joy Comes In The Morning

Brenda Telles

Sing to the Lord, you saints of his; praise his holy name. For his anger lasts only for a moment, but his favor lasts a lifetime; weeping may remain for a night but rejoicing comes in the morning."
Psalm 30:4-5 (KJV)

Have you ever made a mistake which brought tears to your eyes and wreaked havoc in the lives of others? I have been there and done that.

I was living a good life, had a good marriage, a nice home and felt secure. Then I made a selfish decision that caused me to weep tears of sadness for a long time.

King David – who felt secure in his riches and power – also made a selfish decision. However, he realized his waywardness and ran to the Lord for help. When we find ourselves in moments like this, we should do the same. Unfortunately, when we fail to do so, we hurt ourselves and others.

During my time of regret, I searched God's Word and accepted His love and forgiveness.

Becoming self-reliant, self-secure and independent of God

has its consequences. I can relate to that. Even when we stray from God and go our own way, I have learned He is compassionate, forgiving and worthy of our praise.

Even through your mistakes, you can have the favor of God in your life. Though weeping may come at night, remember the joy of the Lord comes in the morning.

Today, my life is stronger and better than ever before.

Just as sure as the sun rises in the morning, so it is with God who reveals Himself to us every day. And when the darkness of our deeds gets illuminated by the goodness of God, we are forgiven and find security in Him.

Lord, no matter how dim things may seem, keep me in your perfect peace no matter what may come my way. May I always remember that You are the restorer of my joy, the refuge and lover of my soul. Amen.

Divine Grief

Christine Lanton

"But we do not want you to be uninformed, brothers and sisters, about those who have died, so that you may not grieve as others do who have no hope.
1 Thessalonians 4:13 (NRSV)

I have to catch my breath every time it happens: The Divine Encounter. You think you're going to a place for a certain reason but, when you get there, you find that God has something very different in mind.

I couldn't escape the irony of this encounter…Two strangers at an event who talked about what God thinks about abortion. We thought we would be talking about the loss of life inside the womb, but we wound up talking about the loss of our child outside the womb.

When you experience the death of a child, one of the hardest questions you will be asked is, "How many children do you have?" It has been a couple of years, but I still choke when I answer this question.

The person asking me doesn't know this is a reminder of my pain, so sometimes I just say "two" to escape the awkwardness.

This night was different. The elderly gentleman who God divinely placed across from me started to tell me why he feels compelled to tell people about the Lord. "Life is short," he said. "We must tell our children and grandchildren about God, that when you leave this life there is a Heaven and it's glorious."

Then, the question came, "Do you have children?" Before I could answer, the man tells me he lost two sons within three years of each other.

I whisper, "My daughter died."

His countenance – and I believe mine as well – changed. We knew we could speak freely about our sadness and speak the name of the one missing at the table.

It was so refreshing to talk about my loss with someone who has been there. God knew this and He brought us together to comfort one another. We grieved in hope. Though sad for the loss, we are hopeful to see our children again.

Thank You, Father for Divine encounters! Help me to give my grief a voice and help me to comfort as I have been comforted. In Jesus' name, amen.

For Such A Time As This

Dawana Quintana

If you keep quiet at a time like this, deliverance and relief for the Jews will arise from some other place, but you and your relatives will die. Who knows if perhaps you were made queen for just such a time as this?
Esther 4:14 (NLT)

Esther was strategically placed in her time, nationality, and family with a divine purpose.

Likewise, each one of us was chosen and intentionally placed by God at this moment in history, with our nationality and in our family. Like Esther, all of us were created with a God-designed destiny to be fulfilled. She chose to fulfil that destiny even at the possible cost of her own life.

Her unique gift was not only her beauty, but obedience. She chose to obey! An entire group of people was spared death by her literally "stepping" into her destiny. She knew if she entered into the king's presence without being called, she could be put to death. Even so, she made her decision out of obedience and selflessness. She elected to view her life as positioned by God. She risked everything to do what God called her to do.

Truly, God has strategically placed YOU where you are today. Position yourself to look who you are to save: a child, a co-worker, a family, a generation. Then obey the voice of God and step into your destiny. It may be at the sacrifice of your comfort, acceptance, or even your very life, but step into it nevertheless. You were created for "such a time as this."

Father, today I choose to step into my destiny. I choose to obey your voice regardless of any risk. I know You have a divine purpose for my life. I recognize You have positioned me exactly where I am. And I choose to walk out your plan by obeying You every day in every way. Amen.

Rollercoaster

DeAnna Lucas

There is no fear in love; but perfect love drives out fear…
1 John 4:18 (NIV)

Growing up, I was deathly afraid of heights. The sheer thought of the unreliability of rollercoasters would send me into panic mode. The unknown outcome from a upside loop or sudden drop would cause me to sit out on every trip to the amusement park. I would feel excluded from the excitement my friends and family were experiencing.

When you have a relationship with Jesus it's much like a rollercoaster. Not because He is inconsistent and all over the place, but because when you say "yes" to Him you're saying "yes" to a beautifully unpredictable adventure.

Are you allowing fear to keep you from what God has for you? When you allow fear to navigate your life, you are saying that trusting Jesus is not enough.

We think He can't handle our weaknesses, our sins and our questions. But He can! You see, the amazing thing about Jesus is He took the first move. His sacrifice on the cross is a clear declaration of His love and devotion to us. Thus, we can stand firm in Him.

Part of our responsibility in this relationship is to step past the fear of the unknown in our journey with the Lord. Easier said than done, but once we do it, many doors open that we never imagined.

How did I overcome my fear of rollercoasters and heights? I stepped foot on the London Eye, fourth largest Ferris Wheel in the world. Talk about a rush of fear! If I had allowed fear to determine my joy that day, I would have missed out on an event of a lifetime few small-town Texas girls get to experience.

The perfect love of Jesus is full of excitement! Can He have your fear in exchange for His love? Can He have your weakness in exchange for His strength? Today, I challenge you to take a baby step in the direction of trusting the Lord with something you're holding on to. Don't let fear win!

Dear Lord, may my desire for your will be greater than my fear. I stand firm in that You go before me and surround me on all sides as I step in trusting You with my current situation and with my future. Amen.

Tell Your Story

Debbie Lucas

And they overcame him by the blood of the Lamb,
and by the word of their testimony;
and they loved not their lives unto the death.
Revelation 12:11 (KJV)

When I first studied Revelation 12:11, I always thought of my testimony as being the moment I believed in Jesus as my personal Lord and Savior. The longer I have lived, I realize that my salvation experience is not only my testimony, but an accumulation of events that I can share of how the Lord has been good to me.

As I ponder God's goodness, I am reminded of the many trials He has brought me through; how He walked with me at all times and never left me. Even when the trials were more than I could bear on my own, God demonstrated His faithfulness. I look back and can testify that He has been with me through every season of my life.

As a women's ministry leader, my greatest desire is to see women encourage one another in the faith. I have experienced that telling of God's goodness can be such an encouragement to other Christian women. 1 Thessalonians 5:11 says, "Therefore encourage one another and build each other up, just as in fact you are doing." No matter how long we have walked with the Lord, we need others to come alongside and encourage us as well.

We live in a world that will get darker before Jesus returns. But, knowing the victory is ours and remembering the victories we have had in the past brings light into the darkness.

Your story is important! Others need to hear about the goodness and faithfulness of our Heavenly Father. You have a unique testimony; you have a personal story to tell.

Thank You, Father, not only for my salvation through the shedding of your blood, but for all that You have brought me through and will in the future. Help me to call to remembrance such times to encourage others and to encourage myself in the faith. I am an overcomer because of who You are and what You have done for me! Amen.

Dare To Hope

Deena Shelton

Yet I still dare to hope when I remember this…
Lamentations 3:21 (NLT)

How often have you heard the verse that comes just after this one in Lamentations? It says, *"The faithful love of the Lord never ends! His mercies never cease. Great is His faithfulness, His mercies begin afresh each morning."*

What an encouraging reminder! What a great inspiration! But what about when you awake in the morning and you don't feel the new mercy this verse promises? It is easy to move on and lose the promise of this passage if we miss the transitioning verse and what comes before it.

The twenty verses before that promise are true lamentations—they are the cry of a heart that has endured devastation, rejection, depression, abandonment and loss. The writer says in verses 17 and 20, *"Peace has been stripped away, and I have forgotten what prosperity is"* … *"I will never forget this awful time, as I grieve over my loss…"*

But it is at the moment that he transitions with a phrase so alive and daring. *"Yet I still dare to hope..."* In the middle of the darkest time, he clings to the truth of God's unending love. That is the fuel that gives him the ability to stare his dark days right in the face and say, *"In spite of you, I will still hope."*

Are you struggling with something that is weighing down your heart and mind? Maybe it is a current relationship, a past hurt from abuse, or a broken heart because of an unfulfilled desire.

God sees you and hears the cry of your heart. He offers you access to His unending love and faithfulness – and those truths transcend what you experience on this earth. You do not have to wait for your situation to change to experience His connection to you and the vehicle for that is your active hope in what you know to be true.

God, even in the middle of my struggle, I choose connection to You. Help me today to be daring and active in my hope in You. Amen.

Faithful Few

Diane Hawkins

Nevertheless, when the Son of Man comes,
will he find faith on earth?
Luke 18:8 (ESV)

I listened to my daughter Shaina as she recounted her story of several college students who had been Christians but no longer identified themselves as believers.   She was somewhat disheartened but thankfully said, "I'm glad you and daddy were there for me when I had questions. It helped me to keep my faith."

She realized that faith is not something that you put on and take off, but rather it is living moment by moment and day by day for the Lord. It is praying that God's kingdom will come and His will be done daily in our lives.

My daughter and I also saw several of her home church friends walk away from their faith and back into the things of the world. These young men and women who once were passionate for God a few years ago, now were no longer interested in Christianity.

At that time, Luke 18:8 came to mind. I asked, "Where are the righteous and why are they not shining? Where are the faithful? Will they continue to be faithful?"

Some start on the Christian path and walk away. However, as children of the Father, we must remain earnest in our walk and fervent in our prayer. We must also continue to believe in the One who sees and knows all. When Christ returns, He will come back for those who have remained faithful.

The beginning of verse 7 states, "And shall not God avenge His own elect, which cry day and night unto Him?" We are encouraged to remain steadfast, no matter what trials, tribulation and persecution come our way. God will rescue His saints! Therefore, we must continue to pray to our Father day and night.

We know our faith will be tried by the life issues we encounter in this world; however, God's power and mercy will keep His elect until the end.

God, help me to remain faithful in the midst of a troubled world, knowing that You are the author and finisher of my faith. Amen.

His Great Care

Helen Lynn

Do not be like them, for your Father knows
what you need before you ask Him.
Matthew 6:8 (NIV)

Many years ago, I stood in my kitchen one Wednesday evening when reality struck! I was a struggling single mom and all I had was peanut butter and jelly, but no bread for my children's lunches the next day.

Payday wasn't until Friday. So, a loaf of bread was a major purchase.

I told the Lord, "I have peanut butter and jelly, but I have no bread." And I knew I had to trust Him to provide for us one more time.

It was our custom on Wednesday nights to attend our evening church activities. As I approached the nursery, I saw my friend Jane. I noticed she appeared emotional and, with tears in her eyes, she handed me a plastic bag. To my amazement, there were two loaves of bread!

She explained that she had been fighting with the Lord all day.

He told her to bring me a loaf of bread, but she struggled because she didn't want to give me something so small and insignificant.

To Jane, it was a small offering – just two loaves of bread – but to me, it was monumental! The bread not only met my need to provide my children's lunches until Friday, but it reminded me what a great God we serve.

Those two loaves of bread have ministered to me many times through the years. That incident built my faith. Thus, in other difficult circumstances, I have been able to stand with faith and assurance knowing that the Lord sees me and He will ALWAYS take care of me. He will do the same for you!

Precious Father, You never overlook us and your provision is never-ending. Thank You for your great care. Amen.

Cheat The World

Holly Frank

Beware lest anyone cheat you through philosophy and empty deceit, according to the tradition of men, according to the basic principles of the world, and not according to Christ.
Colossians 2:8 (NKJV)

My big thinker called out from the back seat, "Why don't we do things like 'they' do?"

I started to answer but stalled for the right words. It's hard to put big ideas into simple words for children. I piggybacked off of the foundations of his faith that we'd been building on for years – the kingdom. It's really quite separate from everything the world presents, isn't it?

The central features are that the Kingdom of God always brings fullness—even when it is correcting or forceful, the outcome is always life-giving.

Think through the natural flow of the systemization of how everything comes and goes, how the world defends itself, schemes for itself, but in the end still gets swallowed up in what Paul called "empty deceit." People work hard to prove themselves only to have the work of proving turn on them and empty them out.

What I mean to say is, the world works really hard to convince others that they are worthy. Worth what? Worth anything that is right in front of you, anything desirable or impressive. But just the work to get whatever it is and then the work to be looked at for it, is in itself the work that tricks you. It's the very thing that makes you feel empty.

If we get cheated about what we've gained through salvation it's not just about us. Oh no, we also cheat the world.

We work instead of receive. We convince others of our worth instead of agreeing with Jesus, and lastly, we go after having a life. We settle down in life, having life achievements- whatever our tradition of men calls them—and we're void. Strong words.

This means others stay blind to everything that will truly fill them up. Philosophizing our way into the system of the world, cheats the world. Maybe the whole world right out of the Kingdom of His beloved Son (Colossians 1:13).

Father, make me keen to watch out for myself. I choose to not get talked into what makes sense–but is still part of a pattern that I don't belong to. I declare that I will not cheat anyone from seeing the Kingdom of Christ, and will not be cheated from it myself. Amen.

Strength And Dignity

Janie Peña

She is clothed with strength and dignity,
and she laughs without fear of the future.
Proverbs 3:25 (NLT)

When I was a little girl, I loved reading books, especially biographies.

Many of these books were about strong women who are now viewed as having played an integral part in American history. Whether it was Clara Barton, Harriet Tubman or Sacagawea (three of my favorites) all demonstrated courage and an understanding that each of us is called to a purpose by our God.

In my own life, I was influenced by a young woman who began her life as a migrant worker in the Rio Grande Valley of Texas. Although she was not able to complete her elementary school years, she still learned to read and write in Spanish and English.

She married the love of her life and together they began a new life far from the Valley to the Plains of Texas. This young woman became a mother after many years of marriage and praying for a child.

Always remembering this child was an answer to prayer, she was never too busy to stop her daily housekeeping chores to play "*las comadritas*" (tea party). She and her child would discuss the issues of the day while sipping make-believe tea together.

These are precious memories for me since I was that little girl and her only child.

My mother did not make the history books but in every way, she was as strong and determined as the women who I read about in the American history books. She taught me that moral character was precious and a gift to be guarded and honored.

Knowing that God had heard her prayers, she raised me in the ways of the Lord always telling me how God had a purpose for my life because I had been a miracle baby.

She believed that life was precious and to be lived fully with gratitude and grace. She taught me not to fear the future but to move forward with the boldness that only God's Word and direction can provide. It is my joy to be called her daughter and to know today she is in the presence of our Lord.

Father, I thank You for the guidance and love of a God-fearing woman, friend and mother. Amen.

Made For Greatness

Jessica Wilson

But you are not like that, for you are a chosen people. You are royal priests, a holy nation, God's very own possession. As a result, you can show others the goodness of God, for he called you out of the darkness into his wonderful light. Once you had no identity as a people; now you are God's people. Once you received no mercy: now you have received God's mercy.
1 Peter 2:9-10 (NLT)

Do you have a dream, a step that God has asked you to take, or a hope that you have boxed up and put away? Maybe you felt like it was silly or it was too late? Many times, we bury those dreams because we feel like we are unworthy and unlikely to carry them out. Or perhaps we have allowed fear to steal those dreams.

It's not too late. The Bible is full of stories of men and women who were not qualified – and even messy – that God used to do incredible things to fulfill His purpose and to change the world.

The enemy would like nothing more than to steal that dream away. He wants to tell you it's too late because he fears what you will do in the future. Know that your dream was planted there by a God who loves you and it is not a coincidence.

When God looks at you, He sees a person chosen to carry out the mission He has called you to do. He sees a person whose redemptive story will be shared with others.

He sees an unlikely person who was made for greatness. Take your dreams and desires back to the place of hope. If He told you to do something, He will give you everything you need to accomplish the plan. If He gave you a promise, He will fulfill. You were made for greatness.

Loving Father, open my eyes to see myself the way You see me. I take the dreams and promises that I have buried, and I bring them back to You, my place of hope. I trust that You will fulfill your promises for You have made me for greatness. Amen.

So Loved

Kelly Mays

But God showed his great love for us by sending Christ to die for us while
we were still sinners.
Romans 5:8 (NLT)

My sister gave me a framed picture for my birthday this year. The picture had the words "So Loved" from Romans 5:8 on a black background with beautiful peonies in pale pink aligned along the bottom of frame.

This was shortly after a tough breakup that left me heartbroken and struggling to understand God's plans for me. Now, a year and a half later, I still don't understand God's plans, but can rejoice in what I do know.

Sadly, I didn't understand the love of my earthly father until I was in my thirties. You see, the love I received from him wasn't what I thought it should be. He worked long hours and was away from home a lot causing me to feel rejected my whole life.

Pastor Greg Hansen, my spiritual father, helped me understand the true meaning of love. I learned that God's love is more than I could have ever imagined – and oh so much more.

Not only that, I learned that God knew the depth of my sin before I ever took my first breath. He also knew the years I would spend in rebellion. He saw the derailment of my life before I had a chance to take the first step off the path.

All the time I had my back and deaf ears to Him, yet He loved me, anyway. His love is so great, He sent Christ to die for me. Every other whisper or shout of love pales in comparison to this love.

When I doubt that I am loveable, I remember this verse. When I think I am unworthy of love, I remember the proof of God's love. It cannot be earned. I will never be good enough. God is simply that loving. Bask in the assurance of that love.

God, You are a good, good father. Thank You for the precious gift of your love. Bring this verse to the forefront of our thoughts when we doubt, we are loved. Amen.

Wait On The Lord

Linda Serrano

But they that wait upon the Lord shall renew their strength; They shall mount up with wings as eagles; they shall run and not be weary; and they shall walk, and not faint.
Isaiah 40:31 (KJV)

On this journey called "life," we are confronted with many varying situations and dilemmas.

If we were to tell our life story, no doubt we would all share very happy moments as well as sad ones. Generally, our perspective is based on our past experiences and beliefs.

As Sisters in Christ, it is our desire to react to negative comments or challenging events in a Christ-like manner. However, in the fast-paced momentum of our lives, we often react too quickly, fail to honor the Lord, and consequently fall into guilt for our behavior.

Recently, when I was confronted with a situation, I was so overwhelmed that I couldn't even react at all! I was distrustful and physically/mentally stressed. If I had reacted out of "past woundedness," I would not have been Christ-like and would not have had peace in the end.

With no other option, I literally "waited on the Lord" and He quickly began to reveal to me how He wanted me to respond to this particular situation. Not only was I able to respond appropriately with God's love, but I received understanding and my strength was renewed as the Scripture says.

His Word says, if we simply (and literally) WAIT on Him, He SHALL renew our strength; we shall mount up with wings as eagles; run and not be weary; and walk, and not faint. What a simple recipe for success to deal with difficult situations in our lives!

Dear Lord, thank You for your Word that is a reservoir of love, wisdom, and truth that we can apply to our everyday lives!
In Jesus' name, amen!

Prescription For Spiritual Toughness

Mary Mendez

Bless the Lord, O my soul: and all that is within me, bless his holy name.
Bless the Lord, O my soul,
and forget not all his benefits…
Psalm 103:1-5 (KJV)

I knew something wasn't quite right when I heard, "Good morning. I am Dr. Cox, your oncologist."

I felt tired and had weird symptoms such as high fever and stiffness at night, then back to normal by morning.

Seven months earlier, my primary physician was unable to diagnose the cause of these symptoms. Now, Dr. Cox informed me that I must begin chemotherapy immediately and would have to have a port surgically attached the first week of June 1992.

What does a person do when faced with this medical condition? Personally, I ran to Psalm 103:1-5 and "forget not all his benefits" caught my attention. Since I was a single parent and a physical education teacher, I knew I was going to need both emotional and physical toughness.

As I studied verse 3 –"Who forgiveth all thine iniquities, who healeth all thy diseases" – I found my HOPE. I knew Jesus had forgiven me of all my sins; therefore, how could I not believe that He heals all my diseases?

Also, I knew I would need protection from the effects of chemotherapy, from weekly blood work, the numerous cat scans and other procedures that would be required. I also leaned on the Word that says, "Who redeemeth thy life from destruction, who crowneth thee with lovingkindness and tender mercies."

As I memorized these verses, as a prescription for my spiritual toughness, I meditated on "who satisfieth thy mouth with good things; so that thy youth is renewed like the eagle's." I desired to be like an eagle so I could fly above this huge storm. Confessing this Scripture aloud and writing it down helped me overcome the most challenging time of my life.

Know that this Psalm is also a PROMISE for you. These BENEFITS are for you. And this TRUTH is for you.

Father, thank You that You keep your promises and that your mercies are new to us every day. In Jesus' name, amen.

Standing On God's Word

Maye Moore

*Be strong and of good courage, fear not, nor be afraid of them: for the Lord
thy God, he it is that doth go with thee,
he will not fail thee, nor forsake thee.
Deut. 31:6 (KJV)*

Every one of us goes through fiery trials and storms in life.
In those times we can look to Jesus for He will never leave us nor
forsake us.

When we allow our emotions to take over, stress grips our
hearts with fear. Fear is the opposite of faith. It is torment from
the enemy. However, the moment we call on Jesus, He is there. No
matter what, He will see us through our storms and trials.

In 2017, I had severe abdominal and chest pains, high blood
pressure and heart palpitations. I sought medical attention and
several tests were performed. The problem was diagnosed, and
the doctor recommended radical surgery. However, I chose not to
have it and decided to fast and pray for healing. Praise God, He
miraculously healed me!

As I went through this difficult time in my life, the Lord Jesus reminded me of the three Hebrew boys in the book of Daniel who were thrown in the fiery furnace because they would not worship the king. But God was with them, even walking around in the fire protecting them.

When the enemy brings opposition, miracles are on the way and the victory is near. You ask, "How is that so?" When you trust and believe, God shows up. That is exactly what these young men did. They trusted God with all their hearts, and He delivered them out of the fire. Be encouraged that all things are possible with God. There is nothing too difficult for Him. When we stand on God's Word, our faith grows as we trust Him.

Our Almighty God, El Shaddai, is aware of your everyday challenges. No need to fret, just rest in the arms of the Father.

Almighty God I turn my eyes upon You. I will trust and not be afraid. You will never abandon me. Thank You for your divine interventions in my life. In Jesus' name, amen.

Dandelion Distractions

Natalia Meltabarger

"I keep my eyes always on the Lord.
With him at my right hand, I will not be shaken."
Psalm 16:8 (NIV)

Oftentimes as we progress in our Christian walk, the enemy plants weeds of discouragement, confusion and even temptation in our minds. They distract us because it doesn't take much for them to grow and choke out all the good things God has planted.

They grow tall and fast and sometimes, like the dandelion, even flower causing us to wonder if they are really all that bad.

Don't be fooled, weeds are weeds. We must allow God's Spirit to expose them and pull them up by the root. This often takes much more muscle than we have in our own strength, so He employs His strength in our weakness.

As I wrote this devotion, things weighed heavy on my heart and mind. Weeds of discouragement quickly tried to make their appearance. I began to think thoughts like "forgotten," "overlooked" and "hopeless." Vines of anxiety and worry threaded through my mind and threatened, "This could overtake you!" I sat down quickly and whispered, "Lord, help me!" and turned on some worship music to find encouragement.

I closed my eyes and asked God to captivate my thoughts. He soon reminded me He lives in me and is greater than the enemy's lies. I declared, "I am not a slave to fear! I will not be overtaken because God provides a way for me. No weapon formed against me will prosper! My hope is in the Lord!"

God's Word is living, active, and it discerns our thoughts and intentions. It is our weed killer!

Father God, I recognize my mind is a battlefield. I surrender myself to You and ask You once again to help me take every thought captive and make it obedient to You. Holy Spirit, thank You for helping me discern your thoughts. Give me your strength in exchange for my own. Help me to keep my eyes on You, knowing that I will not be shaken with You beside me. Amen.

Peace For Jerusalem

Pat Lewis

Pray for the peace of Jerusalem: they shall prosper that love thee. Psalm 122:6 (KJV)

God is not kidding around! He means what He says! And He says in this verse to pray for Jerusalem.

I love Israel and pray for her protection and well-being each day. Furthermore, I pray that the people of Israel will one day come to the knowledge of Yeshua as Savior and Redeemer.

I am not a Jew but my interest in Israel began when I was in college and I had to write a theme paper on a current event. That was the year Israel declared itself a nation and war immediately broke out with the Arab neighbors. My roommate and I listened intently to the radio for days.

We had contentious discussions because of our opposite points of view. My position was that God gave the land to Abraham's descendants, Isaac and Jacob, through covenant and has never taken it back.

A wonderful Bible teacher confirmed the way I felt about that country and broadened my knowledge. He later invited me to participate in mission trips to Israel. And the rest is history.

I have visited that country more than thirty times. It's been my great privilege to share God's promises with the people there and, on some of my trips, teach believers about God's purpose and plan for Israel.

The important thing is that I find my love and will for the land entwined with His love and will. Israel is the only place on earth that He created and that He has reserved for Himself. That is why we pray for the peace of Jerusalem.

We certainly do not pray for Israel to get rich, but to obey and please God. He blesses and rewards us when we pray for that nation.

Precious Lord, because we love and desire to please You, help us realize that the caveats on your many promises are there to guide us into your purpose and plan for our lives. In Jesus' name, amen.

The Enemy's Playground

Patricia Binkley-Childress

*And do not be conformed to this age, but be transformed by the renewal of
your mind, so that you may approve what is the good and well-pleasing and
perfect will of God.*
Romans 12:2 (LEB)

In this age, we are surrounded by television, radio, computers,
and hand-held devices that provide secular music, less-than-
positive news, less-than-wholesome movies and weekly shows and
social media discussions that consume our every waking minute.

Though technology benefits humanity, it is also a perfect
playground for our archenemy Satan. If not used responsibly,
negative outcomes could include distraction, depression, anxiety,
envy, disharmony, pride and apathy. If we adopt the lifestyle of
today's technology culture, we're in danger of being *"conformed to
this age"* and at risk of drowning out the voice of the Holy Spirit.

It is a battle, but it's one we must fight. Daily, we must adopt
an attitude of balance and restriction. God must be first and
foremost. And some things must be eliminated in order to hear
God's voice. Otherwise, we will hear no voice or worse yet, we will

hear lies from the enemy.

God says in Psalm 46:10 (LEB), "Be still, and know that I am God. I will be exalted among the nations; I will be exalted in the earth." We hear and reverence God by being still with no distractions and exalting Him above everything else.

He also says in Philippians 4:8 (ESV), "Finally brothers (sisters), whatever is true, whatever is honorable, whatever is just, whatever is pure, whatever is lovely, whatever is commendable, if there is any excellence, if there is anything worthy of praise, think about these things." We protect our minds from the enemies' lies by filling them with what God defines as good.

Today, let's commit to transformation by renewing our mind God's way instead of the world's way.

Heavenly Father, forgive me for time wasted on technology which is useless for your kingdom and harmful for my mind. Help me to be strong against the temptation to waste precious hours with things that are of no eternal significance. I love and want You to have my undivided attention. In Jesus' name, amen.

Rest

Rachel Wilson

Come to me, all you who are weary and burdened,
and I will give you rest.
Matthew 11:28 (NET)

In all of our lives we have days that are challenging. Even though there are various reasons why we might be feeling overwhelmed, the truth is that Jesus and His Spirit are there for us…they are on call no matter the time or hour.

Being a teacher brings many days when I feel "weary and burdened." In the past, when I needed that moment to vent, I reached out to a neighbor teacher or my husband with the latest story of a back talking second grader. Both these two individuals are excellent listeners and it always eased my mind.

There are other times when I have asked my husband, my mother or a friend for prayer. I have found myself struggling and waiting for their prayer to kick in like some spiritual ibuprofen. It's like I'm expecting God to hear their prayers, wave His wand and I will magically feel better. Please don't misunderstand me. I believe in intercessory prayer and God has answered through the prayer of others....

BUT, in this verse in the book of Matthew, Jesus told his disciples to come to Him and He would give them rest.

Today, I am grateful we have His Spirit who gives us the same rest he offered the disciples. Though our brothers and sisters in Christ can pray for us and provide us support, we can go directly to the source: Jesus.

We must lean on God. During our times of struggle, if even for a few seconds, let's find ourselves at the feet of our Maker, lay our burdens and frustrations down and reach out for His rest. Once we do that then we can be ready to face the cause of our troubles with grace and to bring glory to our Father.

Lord, help me to think of You first when I'm frustrated, tired or overwhelmed. Remind me to give You my burdens and to take on your rest. In Jesus' name, amen.

Keep Practicing

Rebecca Cleere

Keep putting into practice all you learned and received from me—
everything you heard from me and saw me doing.
Then the God of peace will be with you.
Philippians 4:9 (NLT)

The Apostle Paul was an amazing example of a man who gave his all, in pursuit of Christ.

Time after time, Paul speaks about the Lord and encourages anyone who would listen to follow the example of Christ. Paul tells Euodia and Syntyche – who had a disagreement in the church at Philippi – to settle their differences and continually practice the teachings they had learned and received from him.

I love the wording here; the idea of "keep practicing" is continual. However, I believe this teaching is counter intuitive for us in that we often seek the easiest, fastest solutions or a "quick fix." It is not a one and done type of situation. Rather, it is listening, learning and doing.

So how do we start this process of practicing? For me, I think of how much "Jesus loves me this I know for the Bible tells me so."

I sang this song as a child and today I sing it to my children. It's so basic and yet so profound but it's a start.

As we start with the basics, we begin to learn and progress/grow in our walk with the Lord.

I remember in school, I worked hard to master a new concept. Once I had, it was time to move to another. Now, I realize that each mastered skill helped me build and prepare for the next task set before me.

Paul assures us that as we follow his example and practice it, God's peace will be with us. I have found this to be true in my life. I have seen this Scripture come to life in some amazing examples of people who follow God first and then lead others. It is my prayer that I can be this kind of example to others, as well.

God, help me to learn this teaching and become a good student. Place in me a desire to be a lifelong learner and disciple. Thank You for going with me wherever I go. Amen.

Our Deliverer And Healer

Rebecca Joy Hardin

Blessed is the one who considers the poor! In the day of trouble, the Lord delivers him; the Lord protects him and keeps him alive; he is called blessed in the land; you do not give him up to the will of his enemies. The Lord sustains him on his sickbed. In his illness you restore him to full health.
Psalm 41:1-3 (ESV)

I became familiar with this Scripture when my mother was diagnosed with colon cancer that had spread to the tip of her liver. That was a "day of trouble" for our family.

My mother always had a heart of mercy. She brought young women, some with their children, into her home when they had no place to go. She also brought both of my grandmothers to live with her in their later years.

One day while praying for my mother, the Lord brought these verses to my mind. After reading them, I immediately knew that He would restore her to full health. He sustained her through two surgeries and chemotherapy.

That was twenty years ago and today she is ninety-two, going strong and cancer-free.

When you have a "day of trouble" – spiritual, emotional, physical or financial – remember these Scriptures that the Lord is our Healer and Deliverer and, more than that, Jesus is sitting at the right hand of our Father, praying for you.

He will give you your own testimony of His amazing grace, love, power and faithfulness. He is not only your Lord who heals you; He is also your Deliverer.

Dear Father, we lift our hearts to heaven to the Holy One we love. We pray that You send your Spirit, your mercies and your love. We pray that You answer us and glorify your name with mighty works of power to bring our Savior fame. Amen.

Walking In Wholeness

Rhonda Baker

Let it be known to you all, and to all the people of Israel, that by the name of Jesus Christ of Nazareth, whom you crucified, whom God raised from the dead, by Him this man stands here before you whole.
Acts 4:10 (NKJV)

We all are guilty of looking for things to fill us up, be it food for our bellies or feelings for our hearts. We grasp at anything we can plug into the voids we know we have deep down inside.

"You complete me," the famous line quoted by Tom Cruise in the movie *Jerry McGuire*, resonated with women across the board for a reason.

The world offers plenty of things to help us be complete. The aforementioned food and feelings, as well as kids, jobs, money, prestige to name a few. Our flesh will try to snatch any square peg it can grab hold of and force it into the round holes of our longing. However, just like the children's toys, we weren't designed to have square pegs fill round holes.

Like the lame man found in the book of Acts, we are unable to walk as God would have us in our own strength. The square pegs we grab simply become crutches.

They help us appear as though we are walking in wholeness, but as soon as one is knocked out from under us, we fall once again. When one crutch breaks – we grab another. Hobbling along, looking for the one thing that will make a lame man walk free.

Sisters – the One thing is no secret. His name is Jesus.

Peter's declaration in this verse is all should know Jesus.

Jesus – who died for our sins.

Jesus – who God raised from the dead.

Jesus – by whose name alone do any of us stand before the world whole.

And sisters, because of Jesus, we all can be complete!

Jesus, thank You for both seeing and loving us in our lameness. As odd as it may sound, thank You for the lameness because it leads us to You. We praise You for your Word, which shows us how we can walk in wholeness. We thank You it is not dependent on us, for it is by your name alone we stand. Give us courage to walk in your wholeness before this world so we may point them back to You. Amen.

Our Belief Meter

Sharon Shelton

So be subject to God. Resist the devil (stand firm against him), and he will
flee from you.
James 4:7 (AMP)

When I find myself in a battle with the adversary, two things happen: this Scripture comes to mind and I measure my faith through what I call my Belief Meter.

Next, I review my check list. I ask, "Am I subject to God? Have I gone to church? Given tithes and offerings? Prayed? Read my Bible?" These are all wonderful things but none of them, in and of themselves, will cause the devil to flee.

The religion of Islam demands a high calling of faith from its followers. They fast and pray, attend their mosque, read their scripture and bow down toward Mecca. And what good does that do them? Does that make the devil flee? No, the devil does NOT flee because they are not subject to God.

During your battles, check your Belief Meter. On a scale of 1-10 rate your belief system by asking these questions: "Do I believe God's promises will cover my battle? Do I believe in my innermost heart that He will fight this battle? Do I believe I have turned over my cares upon Him? Do I believe He knows and understands my predicament? And do I believe He will deliver me?"

If you believe these things, then you should shout aloud, "I believe, therefore I speak!" My God takes care of me and He perfects all things that concern me. He hears me when I cry out to Him. He's not slow to rescue His children. No foe can withstand His power. And no weapon formed against me can prosper. I am standing on His promises." (You get the picture?)

I believe that thoughts of doubt and fear buckle under confessions of God's Word. So next time you're in a pressure cooker, take the pressure off yourself and your performance meter, and put the pressure on His Word. The devil can stand against a performance meter, but he cannot stand against a Belief Meter that believes God and His Word.

Forever, O Lord, Thy Word is settled in Heaven. In Jesus' name, amen.

God's Oath

Sherry Bridwell

In the same way God, desiring even more to show to the heirs of the promise the unchangeableness of His purpose, interposed with an oath, in order that by two unchangeable things in which it is impossible for God to lie...
Hebrews 6:17-18 (NASB)

An oath is a very serious promise. When God makes an oath, I understand that He will stand by His Word. Keeping promises defines His character. He cannot and will not lie.

One day as I studied this Scripture to gain a better understanding of it, I looked up the definition of the word "oath." I learned it means to witness a person who sincerely intends to do what he says (a guarantee). A good example of this is found in Genesis 12 when God made a promise to Abraham. He told him He would make of him a great nation and a great name; and he would be a blessing to all the nations of the earth. And He kept His promise.

Sometime ago, I received a prophetic word that pertained to a certain injustice that had taken place in my life. I was told by the prophet that God would take care of that injustice. However, I became impatient and decided to take action into my own hands.

Then, I heard the Lord say, "Don't step on my toes, Sherry!"

I wasn't too sure what He meant by that statement. So, I looked at the Cambridge Dictionary and found it means to upset someone especially by getting involved in something that is that person's responsibility. Suddenly, I realized I was trying to do God's work instead of waiting on Him and His timing.

Have you ever wondered what keeps us from receiving from God? It could be that we try to interfere with what He has already promised He would do.

We sometimes allow our trust, disobedience, patience or impatience to dictate our belief to receive or not receive. Faith puts our actions into agreement with His oath.

If we have a God who never gives up on us then why should we give up on Him?

Lord, help me to never "step on your toes" and keep me from interfering with what You have promised You will do. In Jesus' name, amen.

The Beauty Of Discipleship

Sloane Keith

Jesus came and told his disciples, "I have been given all authority in heaven and on earth. Therefore, go and make disciples of all the nations, baptizing them in the name of the Father and the Son and the Holy Spirit."
Matthew 28:18-19 (NLT)

In this verse, we are called to "go and make disciples of all nations." What exactly is a disciple? Simple definition: A follower of Christ.

Furthermore, we are to be students of the Word and to seek wisdom and truth from other Christians. There is something powerful about walking with another sister in Christ on your journey together through discipleship.

In my experiences of being discipled and discipling other young women, one of the benefits is the beauty that comes from simply sharing your struggles and testimonies with one another. We are a work in progress and it is life-giving to know that other sisters in Christ get irritated in traffic or have struggles in relationships, but make every effort to be Christlike.

So, where do you begin? Find a spiritually mature woman who will invest the time to teach, correct, love, counsel and influence you in your walk with the Lord. You will be blessed doing life together as she leads you in humility, truth and sanctification. I promise your life will be better for it!

Our calling, according to Matthew 28:20, says, "...teach these new disciples to obey all the commands I have given you."

What say you? Are you ready to fulfill God's calling on your life?

God, teach me what it means to be a true disciple. Give me the strength and courage I need to disciple others. Teach me how to be more like You through this experience. In Jesus' name, amen.

In Pursuit Of Perfection

Tabitha May-DeBoer

"For though we walk in the flesh, we do not war after the flesh."
2 Corinthians 10:3 (KJV)

Are you warring against yourself? Do you struggle with temptation that feels like a plague and you just can't shake loose from it? You try and you try and there you go again. Still tempted, still wrestling and still getting mad at yourself with no change. Be of good cheer! You are not alone!

We have often heard the old cliché, "No one is perfect." You see, I struggled for years trying to be perfect, praying endlessly and punishing myself for being weak. "But God, I want to be perfect." But I wasn't and I couldn't be. God made us, knows us and accepts us as imperfect. As Christian women, we do not war after the flesh, but after the Spirit.

The referenced verse has been used as a sledge hammer. Like a judge, we hold the gavel in our hand and pronounce harsh verdicts on ourselves. Self-criticism is the secret weapon of the enemy. It is deceitfully disguised as conviction, but its real name is condemnation, guilt and shame. In some women, it can become extreme negative self-talk that births self-hate.

Today, choose to live in Christ, not in your own will power. God knows you need His grace. And guess what else? God knows you are not perfect. That is why He sent the Lord Jesus for you. Stop fighting yourself and give your imperfections to Him.

God, I give myself to You today. I give You my disappointments, my failures and my desires to be in control. Help me to walk in the Spirit and not war in the flesh. Teach me, Lord, how to give You full control and help me embrace your grace for myself. In Jesus' name, amen.

The God Who Never Fails

Vivian Fernand Narcisse

Once I was young, and now I am old. Yet I have never seen the godly
abandoned or their children begging for bread.
Psalm 37: 25 (NLT)

I vividly remember the day when my supervisor told me that I was going to lose my job.

It was during my first post-doctoral studies when a co-worker and I were working on a research project with him. He told us that the research grant funding was not renewed.

This meant that we had to look for another job and I only had two months to find one. On top of that, being an international student, I had other concerns as well. Indeed, the news came unexpectedly and I cried out to God, my Provider, for He was the only One who could help me.

As I held onto His Word, I submitted applications to various schools and research laboratories. I stood on this promise to provide for all my needs.

Moreover, I asked God for the impossible. Specifically, that I would start a new job after the last day of my current job. I reached

out to both my biological and Christian families and asked them
to stand in agreement with me. Sure enough, my Heavenly Father
came through and miraculously provided a new job for me, just as
I asked Him.

Today, you may be facing a financial burden, or have lost your
job or you are looking for another one. Please remember that you
are serving a good and faithful Father who never fails to provide
for His children.

Call out to Him. Cry out to Him. Remind Him of His
promises in His Word and stand upon them. Make these promises
your own. When you humble yourself, you will see your God at
work in your life.

Therefore, be encouraged when you seek God's help because
He hears the cries of those in need (Psalm 69: 32-33). God loves it
when His children trust Him. He is always at work for us behind
the scenes; all we have to do is call upon Him.

*My dear Father, I thank You for being true to your Word and I can stand
upon your promises. Thank You for your faithfulness and for always coming
through for me when I have called upon You. Thank You for being my
Provider. In Jesus' name, amen.*

Divine Intervention

Vivian Bustillos Keith

*Immediately he arose, took up the bed, and went out in the presence of them all and glorified God, saying,
"We never saw anything like this!"*
Mark 2:12 (NKJV)

When was the last time you needed a miracle from Jesus? Throughout the New Testament we find He performed hundreds of miracles.

One morning I heard a teaching on the paralytic man in Mark 2:1-10. As I took notes, I began to visualize the event. The house, that belonged to Peter, was so packed that there was "no more room even outside the door" (vs. 2).

The people had heard about His miracles and every time He was in Capernaum, He drew a crowd. There was a paralyzed man who also wanted to see Jesus but was unable to do so because of the crowd. However, he was so desperate that he found four friends to carry him and lift him to the top of the roof. (He must have been a large man because it took four men to carry him!)

What happens next is astounding. The men began to dig a hole through the roof and you know that was no easy job! Can you see pieces of the ceiling falling on Jesus and the others? What amazes me is that Jesus did not get upset. Instead, He was impressed with their faith and once he was lowered, He healed the paralyzed man!

I have several questions for you today? How desperate are you for a miracle? And what are you willing to do to get it?

These men had obviously heard of Jesus' healings in Capernaum which stirred up their faith. They knew Jesus was in town. Look at all the hard work they performed to get their friend to Jesus. And that, my sisters, is DESPERATION! As a result, Jesus responded and performed a divine intervention!

Faith plus the Word of God equals a miracle! Put your trust in Him and declare His Word over your situation. Jesus acts on your faith. He is the same today, yesterday and forever. He has never stopped performing miracles.

Maybe we don't see these types of miracles today because we aren't desperate. Remember, desperate people do desperate things.

Lord, You are my God, my King and my everything. Help me to be more desperate for You. In Jesus' name, amen.

Don't Yield To Fear

Alaina Strait

While Jesus was still speaking to the woman, someone came from Jairus'
house and told him, "There's no need to bother the Master any further. Your
daughter has passed away. She's gone." When Jesus heard this, he said,
"Jairus, don't yield to your fear. Have faith in me and she will live again."
Luke 8:49-50 (NLT)

How often do we yield to our fears or circumstances that surround us? There are times when we let fear creep in because of what we see, hear or feel.

Losing a child can be considered one of the most horrific experiences imaginable. In Luke 8, Jairus, a religious ruler, learned that his daughter passed away. I can't imagine what he felt upon hearing those words. That was a moment of impact. Jesus knew what he was feeling and told him not to be afraid but to believe.

Jesus lovingly tells Jairus not to fear, but to have faith in Him. I can see the love and compassion in Jesus' eyes as He spoke these words.

I am sure the moment Jesus spoke, Jairus was moved by His words which always bring comfort and wholeness.

I need to be reminded not to yield to fear. Furthermore, I must exercise faith and believe that regardless of the circumstances, my life is in His hands. God knows exactly where I am and I choose to believe He is going to work everything for my good.

When fear comes knocking at your door, remember this Scripture and say, "I will not yield to fear today. I choose to have faith in Jesus." Just as the sun explodes from behind the rain clouds, just as quickly, worship can take you from fear to faith.

"When they arrived at the house, Jesus allowed only Peter, John, and James – along with the child's parents – to go inside. Jesus told those left outside, who were sobbing and wailing with grief, 'Stop crying. She is not dead; she's just asleep and must be awakened.' They laughed at him, knowing for certain that she had died. Jesus approached the body, took the girl by her hand, and called out with a loud voice, 'My sleeping child, awake! Rise up!' Instantly her spirit returned to her body and she stood up." (Luke 8:51-56)

Father, thank You for the words You speak to us and for bringing peace when we experience fear. We acknowledge Jesus as the Prince of Peace and we choose to trust and have faith in Him. Amen.

Kingdom Life

Allison Wolfe Cunningham

For the kingdom of God is not a matter of eating and drinking, but of
righteousness, peace and joy in the Holy Spirit.
Romans 14:17 (NIV)

I recently had to start wearing glasses. It has taken some intention and thought to learn to put them on but what a difference they make! What was blurry comes into full view. Without corrective lenses, I can see but the clarity I need is only realized when I put on the glasses. The Bible encourages us to do the same in our spiritual life. Matthew 6:33 instructs us to seek first the kingdom of God. Like glasses over our eyes, we should see the kingdom first.

Most of us view our lives by circumstances and what we can see right in front of us. The Scriptures invite us to a clarified perspective by looking at the King. When we focus on the King, He brings us into right relationship with Himself. He reveals His heart and nature. A right relationship with Jesus is where you find peace and without peace you will never experience joy.

God's desire is for His kingdom rule to be established on the earth and it happens through the hearts of His people. Our souls are comprised of our mind, will and emotions. Submission of our soul to King Jesus is how we experience the Kingdom of God which is righteousness, peace and joy in the Holy Spirit. When we yield our will to the King, we receive His righteousness.

Laying down our sinful nature and desires at the cross allows for Christ to become the leader of our lives. When Christ leads, He accompanies us in peace. Jesus is the Prince of Peace and He promises to keep our minds in perfect peace when our hearts are stayed on Him. (Isaiah 26:3)

Guilt and shame have no place in the Kingdom. Through relationship with the King and peace presiding over our minds, joy overflows. Jesus promises to give us His joy when we stay connected to him. (John 15:11)

Living in the Kingdom means our minds, wills and emotions are yielded and covered! This is the fullness of life to which Christ calls us. Righteousness, peace and joy in the Holy Spirit!

God, let your Kingdom come on the earth through my life as I yield my soul to You. In Jesus name, amen.

To Whom Will I Listen?

Andrée Elliott

*Do not listen to Hezekiah! Thus says the king of Assyria, Make an
agreement with me by tribute and come out to me, then each man eat of
his own vine and everyone of his fig tree and everyone drink the waters of
his cistern until I come and take you away to a land like your own land, a
land of grain and wine, a land of bread and vineyards, a land of olive oil
and honey, so you can live and not die. Do not listen to Hezekiah when he
persuades you saying, The LORD will deliver us!*
II Kings 18:31 (ONMB)

Note the ploy of Judah's enemy: He speaks to the people. He
entices them to make an agreement with him. He promises them
abundance. And he speaks words of doubt to try to convince them
that the LORD cannot be trusted.

Other Scriptures reveal the same strategy: Genesis 3:4-5, "And
the serpent said to the woman, 'You will not surely die, for God
knows that in the day you eat of it, then your eyes will be opened
and you will be like God, knowing good and bad.'"

Or what about Matthew 4:8-9? "Again the devil took Him
[Jesus] to an exceedingly high mountain and showed Him all the

kingdoms of the world and their glory and said to Him, 'I shall give all these things to You, if after You fall on Your knees You would pay homage to me.'"

Notice Satan's demands in all these verses: Listen to me, and you will not die; pay tribute or homage to me, and I will give you all you desire; trust me, do not trust GOD.

But Jesus says this about the devil in John 8:44: "truth is not in him" and "he is the father of lies." Like Adam and Eve, like the people of Judah, and like Jesus, we have a choice as to whom we listen to and in whom we trust.

Father, thank You for revealing Satan's strategies to deceive us. Thank You, Jesus, that You came to give us abundant life and that You are trustworthy and faithful. We choose to resist the enemy and to put our trust in You.
Amen.

Worship In Weakness

Beth Collins

But he said to me, "My grace is sufficient for you, for my power is made
perfect in weakness."
2 Corinthians 12:9 (NIV)

Are you facing a trial that has you feeling weak and overwhelmed? The Apostle Paul encourages us to boast in our weaknesses. I don't know about you, but when I'm walking through something hard to endure, I just want it to go away! And I definitely don't want to boast in it! That is completely opposite to what I feel like doing.

During a recent trial in my life, I felt so weak I could hardly trust the Lord anymore. I remember pouring out my heart to Him through worship and surrender in the midst of my weakness. And I began a campaign on Satan and his lies through helping others gain victory in the very area I was being attacked.

One day, the Holy Spirit reminded me of how Paul asked the Lord (actually begged Him) to take the "thorn in the flesh" away from him. But the Lord said, "My grace is sufficient for you, for My strength is made perfect in weakness." Paul goes on to say that he is content with his sufferings "…for when I am weak, then I am strong."

We do not know what Paul's thorn was or why God did not take it away. However, he chose to trust God for he knew that His grace would be sufficient for him.

I don't know what thorn you may currently have in your life. But I know if you choose today to worship and lean on God, His strength will be perfect. You can trust Him with your pain. And He will always be faithful.

God, I know You have a purpose and a plan for my life. As I walk through pain in my life, I choose to trust and worship You in the face of adversity. And I surrender the outcome to You. Amen.

Taking Responsibility

Brenda Telles

I can do everything through him who gives me strength.
Philippians 4:13 (NIV)

Paul learned the secret of being content in any and every situation. Whether he had little or much, he confessed this particular verse, "I can do everything through him who gives me strength." He had no desire to compare himself others. But, how often do we fall into that trap and compare ourselves to those around us.

"If only I had the big house, lots of money, the perfect children and husband, then I would be happy. When I compare myself to others, my perspective can become skewed."

As a result, this comparison can cause us to feel insecure and lose our perspective of who we are in Christ.

Where is the peace in all this? There isn't! That's why we need to learn to trust God and believe who He says we are. The more we trust Him, the more familiar we become with the blessed peace that He gives.

If you find yourself with this comparison mindset, I encourage you to go the Lord and ask Him to help you see others through His eyes.

Accept your identity in Christ! Ask the Holy Spirit to help you find your security in Him and only compare yourself to Jesus. Then rely on Him to give you the strength to be more like Him. It is the power of the Holy Spirit that brings change in our lives.

Love people who and where they are.

The Scripture tells us we are fearfully and wonderfully made and God sees us as being perfect in Christ. That's God's measuring stick for us to live by without comparing ourselves to others.

May we always give thanks to the Lord for giving us the strength to do everything He asks us to do and have His eternal perspective.

Lord, I choose to surrender all that I am for your glory. Thank You for the assurance that You will strengthen me and that You will never leave me nor forsake me. Teach me to love others as You do. Make me willing to live according to your will every day. Help me to stay focused on eternity and not that which is temporal. Amen.

Feel, Then Kneel

Christine Lanton

…And if you extract the precious from the worthless,
you will become My spokesman.
Jeremiah 15:19 (NASB)

Have you ever felt lonely in a room full of people? Has your heart been broken over and over again because that loved one would not listen to you? Do you find yourself asking God, "Why me? I've done everything you told me to do!"

The prophet Jeremiah also found himself in a predicament like this.

Jeremiah 15 will always have a special place in my heart. It was the first time I opened my Bible and the words jumped off the page and described my evening! A friend asked me to come to a party and I knew God wanted me to go.

As the night progressed, so did the alcohol and inappropriate conversations. I felt God's heavy hand on me. I stuck out like a sore thumb. I was sober and not laughing at the jokes –different from everyone in the room. I thought, "Here I am doing the right thing but everyone is making fun of me. Jeremiah calls it "bearing reproach."

Feeling rejected and lonely, I went home that night angry at God and my friend! The "why me pity party" began with many tears. Thankfully, I picked up my Bible and as I read the Word, the Word read me.

I cried because I knew God was speaking to me. I cried because I love His Word. I cried over my disappointment and rejection and for the salvation of the people that were at the party. Bingo! I went from being offended to being amended. That was the reason that I was in that room that night.

The Lord had my attention and then He said, "If you extract the precious from the worthless...you will be my spokesman." This became a call on my life and something I am reminded of daily.

Our feelings are instructive, but they never give us the entire picture. So, whenever hurtful feelings rise up, we can remind ourselves to extract and remove the precious things from the filthy. When we do this, God will use us.

Jesus, discouragement is an ongoing battle, but thank You for helping me focus on your promise instead of my feelings and reminding me that when I kneel, I can heal. In Jesus' name, amen.

The Glory Filler

Dawana Quintana

For the earth shall be filled with the knowledge of the glory of the Lord, as the waters cover the sea.
Habakkuk 2:14 (KJV)

Can you imagine the people of every tribe, tongue and nation being filled with the knowledge of the glory of the Lord?

Can you imagine your entire city being led to Christ and walking in the light of His Word?

Can you see your place of employment as a genuine marketplace ministry?

Do you long for the day when the glory of the Lord so completely overwhelms your church that people are engrossed in His presence and radically changed into His likeness?

How can you see this? What can you do? You must be filled with the Holy Spirit and sit in His presence. You must learn to tune your spiritual ears and learn to recognize His voice. When you do this, He will be a part of your everyday life.

We must open up our hearts and say, "POUR OUT YOUR GLORY." Why is it important that He pour out His glory on us?

It is so we can share it and become vessels to carry it.

What happens is that when we are filled with the Holy Spirit, everywhere we go, even without saying a word, His glory pours out on those around us. As He pours into us, we in turn pour out onto others.

Our purpose and plan are to be about the Father's business as He fills the earth with His glory and allows the Holy Spirit to be the Glory Filler!

Father, today I choose to be in your presence. Open my heart and spiritual ears to hear You. Fill me up to overflowing. Let your presence and glory shine through my life that those around me will encounter You! Fill the earth with your glory, Lord! Amen.

Vision

Debbie Lucas

A man's heart plans his way, but the Lord directs his steps...
Proverbs 16:9 (NKJV)

Vision boards can be fun! They turn your thoughts and dreams into reality.

In January of 2019, several of my family members got together and we created them.

We didn't make them expecting they would cause something magical to happen. We created them to do exactly what the name says: a board with our dreams for what we were believing.

We began by digging through magazines to help us find the appropriate photo for each of our vision or dream.

My board consisted of couples vacationing together, women exercising and full of life, cruise ships and travel destinations. The challenge was to find more important visuals such as: serving others, trusting God, having more faith, being more like Jesus and so on. Since I was unable to find any of the above, I had to write them on my vision board.

However, there are times when our thoughts may start to

wander and we lose sight of God's vision for our lives. Romans 12:2 is a great reminder not to be conformed to this world but to renew our minds that we may prove what is good, acceptable and perfect will of God.

Though this family activity was fun and enjoyable and we may have had our own grand ideas, God sees the bigger picture. He has a better plan than we could ever imagine and certainly more than we could ever put on a vision board.

God promises us in Jeremiah 29:11, "For I know the plans I have for you declares the Lord, plans to prosper you and not to harm you, plans to give you a hope and a future." And, in Proverbs 16:9, "A man's heart plans his way, but the Lord directs his steps."

Father, I thank You that your thoughts toward me and my future are good. I ask You to continue to direct my steps, so that I will follow You all the days of my life. Amen.

Waiting Well

Deena Shelton

So Samuel took the horn of oil and anointed him in front of his brothers,
and from that day on the spirit of the Lord came powerfully upon David.
Samuel then went to Ramah.
1 Samuel 16:13 (NIV)

When we think of God's plan for our lives, we often do so with our human minds in a basic, two-step process: God will guide me to His plan and then I will do it.

Sometimes, we feel like God has given us a picture of what He wants for our lives, but we get discouraged if we do not see it happen quickly. It's easy to get disheartened if we miss God's ultimate plan for us to walk closely in relationship with Him as we become more like Him and ultimately influence those around us for His purposes.

When we read a Scripture like the one above and think that God revealed his calling to David, prepared him and then he became king, we wonder why His plan for us isn't coming to pass.

After anointing him, Samuel left and David stayed home and went back to work doing the very thing he was doing before the anointing. Years passed as he protected the sheep, killed Goliath and experienced difficult trials.

After moving into the palace to serve King Saul, David returned intermittently to his father's house to fulfill his duties and tend sheep.

Can you imagine David's day-to-day thought processes as the decades passed before his calling was fulfilled? Read Psalms and you will see the emotional rollercoaster he experienced!

What does God want us to experience while we wait on Him? He wants to help us gain new strength (Isaiah 40:31), give us time to seek Him (Lamentations 3:25), transform us (1 Peter 5:10) and grow intimate with us (Psalm 40:1-2).

What if we stopped concentrating only on the end goal and focused on the parts of the journey that will move us closer to it? What if we were to prioritize seeking Him, growing closer to Him, finding new strength from Him and being transformed by Him? It could make all the difference in the world.

Lord, help me see the ways You are using me today as You prepare me for the future. Amen.

The Restorer Of Life

Diane Hawkins

*Then Naomi took the child and laid him
on her lap and became his nurse.
Ruth 4:16 (ESV)*

My granddaughter grabbed her great-grandfather by the hand and led him around the backyard of his house saying, "Pawpaw, come on."

She was curious about the things around her and he happily obliged her curiosity as she led him here and there.

"Look, Pawpaw."

"What's that, Pawpaw?"

"Sit, Pawpaw."

"Pick me up, Pawpaw."

He listened and responded to her as best he could, trying to understand the language of this inquisitive three-year-old.

God often uses my grandchild to refresh my father. He is eighty-four, but when my granddaughter comes to see him, she challenges him to do things with her. She allows him to see the world through an innocent child's eye. Every blade of grass, bug or rock is a mystery to her. She enjoys spending time with him and her visits give him joy and cheers up his soul. He can't help but smile.

After they had walked together, my dad sat down and my granddaughter crawled into his lap and lay her head on his chest.

My father's relationship with my granddaughter reminds me of the story of Naomi who also had a grandchild.

If you read her story, you will see that she could have given up on ever having a grandchild, but God had a different plan to give her a grandson who would restore her, even in her old age. The women in Ruth 4:14-15 also recognized that the grandchild would be a restorer of life and would nourish Naomi.

Like Naomi's grandson, God also had a plan for His own son, Jesus. God sent Him to be a restorer of life. He brings back to life that which is hopeless and dead.

He says to the dead, "Arise!" and to the sick, "Get up!" God gave his Son to give us life, joy and peace, but we must accept His gift. Jesus desires to nourish and strengthen us and sent the Holy Spirit to fulfill this purpose.

Let us remember that no matter what happens in our lives, God has a plan for us: To show His power and goodness by redeeming His people.

Father, thank You for sending your Son and giving us life through Jesus Christ. Amen.

Prompted To Pray

Helen Lynn

…The effectual fervent prayer of a righteous man avails much.
James 5:16 (NKJV)

Recently, my medical doctor recommended a cardio workup. After several tests, I returned to obtain the results, fully expecting all was well.

To my surprise, I was informed there was 75 to 95 percent blockage in my arteries. The doctor instructed me to go to the hospital for a heart catheterization and possible stent placement that very afternoon.

As a woman of faith and believing in the power of prayer, I talked with my children and texted several close and trusted prayer partners. As I was being processed in the Admitting Office, a dear friend called me.

She had received my prayer request and immediately the Lord prompted her to pray for me. Though it was a quick, powerful and anointed prayer, she prayed with boldness and confidence.

Thereafter, I was transferred to the Cath lab for the procedure where the doctor asked me to view the large screen monitor in the room. He showed me the pictures of my heart and I was astonished to hear him say, "Your heart is perfect! You have absolutely NO blockage at all."

What a miracle!

Afterwards, I wondered if the doctor had made a mistake. How was it possible to go from a high percent blockage to zero blockage in just a couple hours? I remembered that I had seen about forty pictures from the chemical stress test that clearly indicated my heart problem.

I praise the Lord and give Him honor and glory for watching over me and protecting me when I didn't even know I was in danger. I am thankful for faithful praying friends that are sensitive to the Holy Spirit and willing to be obedient to follow through with bold, effective, confident, powerful prayer based on the Word of God.

My story is a testimony that reveals the power of prayer. Do not hesitate to reach out to your circle of Christian women who will stand in agreement with you for God's healing power.

Thank You, Father God, for your faithfulness in our time of need. In Jesus' name, amen!

Still Growing Up

Holly Frank

Therefore, let us, as many as are mature, have this mind;
and if in anything you think otherwise,
God will reveal even this to you.
Philippians 3:15 (NKJV)

When we read the book of Philippians, we find that the Apostle Paul is humble and gracious. A couple of times he mentions that he's still listening to the Holy Spirit, still growing and still attaining the fullness of Christ (1:6, 3:12).

The point being that while Paul talks about wanting to go home to Heaven to be with Christ, he doesn't yet think of himself as fully matured in Christ.

What expectation do you have about maturity? What goals do you set for yourself? What is the standard of biblical knowledge you expect? What's your pace in the good works you do? How about your impression of impressing other believers?

Do you pump yourself up with positive mantras and declarations in the morning? Do you make sure your voice is heard in your Life Group so no one wonders if you're close to God? Can you keep yourself from pointing out the shortcomings of others? Are you wondering what God thinks of you?

Sweetheart, calm down. If you're thinking something inaccurate, He will steer you into truth. If you have a habit that brings others pain, He will give you many gentle opportunities to break that habit before it gets out of hand.

If you can't memorize the address of a Scripture, He is content that the words will be written on your heart. He's calm about the rate of your spiritual growth and you can be, too. He grows you up, and that's that. You are not responsible for your rate of growth; you are responsible to say yes to Him.

Father, help me remember that my authority in the earth is made known by saying yes to You. You want my obedience not my sacrifice. Keep in the forefront of my brain that my freedom in Christ is to grow at your pace and in your ways. I want to enjoy my life and the seasons of it. I choose not to be afraid of missing You simply because I know how to rest. Amen.

Wings

Janie Peña

Keep me as the apple of the eye;
Hide me in the shadow of Your wings.
Psalm 17:8 (NASB)

Several years ago, my mother was very ill in the hospital and was given a diagnosis all of us will hear one day – all has been done and the time to leave this earth is near.

While I was heartbroken and struggling with the fear of losing my wonderful mother, she proceeded to prepare me for that moment. We prayed together and hugged and were comforted by knowing where her final destination would be and knowing we would see each other again.

Blessed with a strong church family, the sister of one of my mom's friends requested the Minister of Pastoral Care from her church visit my mom. He came every week and would pray for her and share God's Word. Mother and I both were appreciative and comforted.

One evening I arrived to find a card on my mother's tray with the Scripture, "Keep me…under the shadow of thy wings." (Psalm

17:8) I asked her about it and she told me our new friend, the minister, had stopped by and shared the card with her. She shared with me how it gave her great comfort to know that she was under the wings of God our Father.

The next day the card was still on her tray and when she was able to go home it remained at her bedside. Even when she returned to the hospital one final time, the card traveled with her until she passed to be with the Lord.

I have kept that card and after reading Scriptures which follow this verse, my eyes were opened to the comfort it must have brought to my mom – and to all of us. In verses 6 and 7, the writer tells us God will incline his ear to hear us and give His loving-kindness to those who trust Him.

Thus, the message of this Scripture is the assurance of God's love and protection over His children. Nothing is more intimate than the embrace of our Father under His wings and knowing we are the apple of His eye! Forever grateful and comforted by this verse.

Thank You, Lord, for your Word which speaks to us clearly and brings us comfort and assurance in times of difficulty and pain. Amen.

No Excuses

Jessica Wilson

Fear not, for I am with you; be not dismayed, for I am your God; I will strengthen you, I will help you,
I will uphold you with my righteous right hand.
Isaiah 41:10 (NIV)

Often when we know God is calling us to take a next step, we begin to question ourselves and sometimes even God. You may ask questions like, "Who am I to lead this project? To teach this class? To interview for this new position?" We are quick to make excuses.

Think of Moses. God said, "I am sending YOU to go to Pharaoh, to lead the Israelites out of Egypt." But in Exodus 3:11, Moses asks, "Who am I?"

I am sure in that moment standing in front of the burning bush, hearing God's voice and the words he spoke, Moses' past came flooding back to him. He began to question his ability, his worth and shame from the past. Moses was unsure of himself, but God was sure of Moses. God chose a man with a past to do something great.

God responds to Moses in Exodus 3:12 by saying, "I will be with you. And this will be the sign to you that it is I who have sent you: When you have brought the people out of Egypt, you will worship God on this mountain."

Moses questioned himself, but God responded by telling him that He would be with him. God worked out all the details and gave Moses everything he needed to fulfill His plan. Moses almost let his weakness become his stumbling block.

Is there something right now that you are allowing to be your stumbling block? If so, do not fear, instead trust God. He will help and strengthen you.

Embrace God's promises in your life. God calls you to greatness. If God spoke it, He will do it, if He promised, He will fulfill. No excuses, stand in His promises and move forward. You have something GREAT to do!

Father, I trust your plan and what You are calling me to do. As I move forward in this next step, I stand on your promises. No more excuses! You are enough and You will fulfill. Amen.

Tears In Your Bottle

Kelly Mays

You have collected all my tears in your bottle.
Psalm 56:8 (NLT)

This collecting of tears is specific to sorrows. How close does one need to be to catch someone's tears? Right there, within reaching distance. God is with us in every moment of sorrow, mourning with us. Weeping with us. Loving us and having compassion on us.

I have known so many beautiful people with more than their fair share of sorrow. And, oh, the tears they have cried. Loss of loved ones. Rape. Divorce. Incest. Brutal attacks of domestic violence. Babies that will never be held. Heartbreak. Rejection. Children who have strayed from God. Unfaithful spouses. Cruel words. Abandonment. Innocence stolen. And so many more.

Dear sister, you know your sorrow and the tears that flowed from that sorrow. God caught every single one.

In learning to recover from things in my past, I was told to ask God, "Where were you when this happened?" How completely does this verse answer that question? He was close enough to capture my tears and He will be close enough to capture yours.

I asked God, "What do you do with our tears?"

He showed me a picture of me sitting covered in ashes. Everything was gray, no color, no sun shining. He poured my tears out over me. The ashes were washed away. The pain, loneliness, heartbreak and sadness were all gone. The sun started shining. Rich, vibrant colors were restored. My life was rejuvenated and everything was beautiful once again. What a beautiful picture!

Father, your love for us has no beginning and no end. Your compassion is without fail, and You are in every moment with us. You never leave us alone in the sorrowful moments of this life. You are close enough to touch every aspect of our sorrows, right down to collecting our tears. Help my sisters to know exactly where You are in their moments of sorrow. Catching their tears. Amen.

This Little Light Of Mine

Mary Mendez

But I say to you who hear: Love your enemies,
do good to those who hate you. Bless those who curse you,
and pray for those who spitefully use you.
Luke 6:27-28 (NKJV)

Has anyone ever made an untrue comment about you? It could have been a co-worker, ex-spouse or family member. In the Old Testament, Joseph was accused of raping the wife of Potiphar, his master. Moses was accused of bringing the children of Israel out of the wilderness to die. And David was accused of trying to dethrone King Saul.

Initially, it is quite natural to ponder the thought of retaliation. But we need to adhere to what Scripture says.

After reading this verse, the word "spitefully" stood out. The dictionary defines it as "caused by malice." I am not one to judge the intent of someone's heart. Their remarks may sound mean-spirited, cutting and hateful. However, I tell myself that I have to be in agreement with God's Word. It's a decision that only I can make; a moment by moment choice to walk in the flesh or in the

Spirit.

I have been a physical education teacher for many years. I once had an experience with a young teacher who made a false statement about me. I could have confronted her and set her straight. Instead, I began to pray for her. The Holy Spirit revealed to me that she did not know what she had done. I asked God to bless her with wisdom and knowledge and to illuminate the truth to her.

Sooner or later, I knew that I would run into this teacher. And I did. Here was the moment of truth. I greeted her, asked how she was doing and offered my assistance.

Did I pass the test that day? How did I view her at that moment? I remembered that hurt people can and will hurt other people. I don't know when her wounding occurred, but I do know that I could be a light to her. This little light of mine, I am going to let it shine.

Choose to be in agreement with God's Word and love. Do good. Bless and pray for others.

Heavenly Father, help me always to remember to be a light to everyone around me. In Jesus' name, amen.

Sweet Communion

Maye Moore

I love them that love me;
and those that seek me early shall find me.
Proverbs 8:17 (KJV)

One day when I was seeking the Lord, I discovered the key to intimacy with Him.

He revealed this key when I made a decision to wake up early every morning to surrender my mind to Him, making sure it was clear and free from distractions. I committed my day to Jesus, the lover of my soul, and gave Him first place in my life.

Oh, the joy of seeking and experiencing His daily presence and spending time in His word captured my heart and mind.

If you will seek Him with your heart you will find Him. Jesus, the Bridegroom, desires you to come into His Holy presence.

Early one morning God gave me Isaiah 50:4 which says, "The Lord hath given me the tongue of the learned, that I should know how to give a word in season to him that is weary: he wakeneth morning by morning, he wakeneth mine ears to hear as the learned." As I confessed this verse, the Holy Spirit drew me to

Himself.

Today, as I pour out my love, my prayers rise to the Lord as incense like a sweet-smelling aroma. I love reading His Word during this time of fellowship. There is nothing like worshipping at the feet of Jesus for it is there that I can experience a deep intimacy with the Father.

This sweet communion forever changed my life.

Worship + His Word = Faith. Remember, faith comes by hearing and hearing by the Word of God. These biblical principles prepare us to share the good news with others as the Holy Spirit leads us to speak an encouraging word to someone in need of the Father's love and compassion.

Heavenly Father, I come to You with a thankful heart. I want to know You more and more and bask in your presence! In Jesus' name, amen.

Help My Unbelief

Natalia Meltabarger

What do you mean, "If I can?" Jesus asked.
Anything is possible if a person believes."
Mark 9:23 (NLT)

At one point or another we all struggle with unbelief. We counteract our faith by reminding God about time constraints as if He doesn't know, and politely request an immediate response. Worry and fear vie for our attention and often create anxiety-driven, self-made plans.

Mark 9 tells us about a father whose son was plagued by an evil spirit. He was desperate to see his son set free. In verse 24, the boy's father exclaims, "Have mercy on us and help us if you can!"

Jesus' reply literally made my heart jump! "What do you mean 'if I can'?" Jesus asked. "Anything is possible if a person believes."

You see, no one has the authority to say such things but our Savior, the one who has taken sin to task and conquered fear and death. Finally, I considered the father's reply in verse 24. "The father instantly cried out, 'I do believe but Lord help me overcome my unbelief.'"

His spirit's response was belief, but he was still challenged with unbelief. What happened next was the show-stopper for me! Jesus rebukes the evil spirit and commands it to come out and the boy is set free.

We often face situations in our lives that are beyond our control. We can bring them to the Lord initially expressing our belief.

However, what happens as we wait is crucial. Just like this boy's father, we must address unbelief before it has the opportunity to cross the threshold of our minds. We can remember Jesus' response, *"If I can?"* and trust His authority over timing, circumstance and even unbelief.

Lord, please help me with my unbelief. My difficult circumstances are not greater than the miracle worker I know You to be. Remind me today that nothing is impossible for You. Help me trust your timing, your authority and your will. Amen.

Through An Intercessor's Eyes

Pat Lewis

I exhort therefore, that first of all, supplications, prayers, intercessions and giving of thanks be made for all men...
1 Timothy. 2:1 (KJV)

The Lord has always encouraged me to look at the big picture in every situation. Seeing the big picture is important but seeing it through God's eyes is more important.

There are a lot of things about our culture that affect each of us and are very disturbing.
Morality is at a new low. What can we do about it? This particular Scripture is certainly a starting place.

Some people say, "I can't pray for such and such a people." And I respond, "Sure you can!"

You can pray for revelation...for a Damascus Road experience... or for the Holy Spirit to reveal the truth to them. James 5:6, says, "...the effectual fervent prayer of a righteous man availeth much."

Remember how the Prophet Elijah fervently prayed and it did not rain for three and a half years? You may be thinking that there is no way your prayers will be heard like Elijah's. Oh, yes, they will because he was a mere man like you and me. You see, dear friend, it was not a man performing the miracle but rather it was the anointing power of God flowing through him.

Today, we hear such discouraging news on television, the Internet and every type of social media. Why not start praying over these media? As outrageous as it may sound, God is still on His throne and who knows what might be accomplished by our prayers!

Another way to pray is to ask God to do something through you or to reveal what He wants you to do. In my walk with the Lord, through intercession, I have experienced many answered prayers. You will be surprised at what happens when you make yourself available to Him.

Dear Lord, thank You for your many blessings in our lives. We offer them back to You to use as You will to restore Godly relationships to this nation. "Here am I… send me." Open the door of your will for me for that is my desire. In Jesus' name, amen.

Uneven Ground

Patricia Binkley-Childress

Then you will walk in your way securely,
And your foot will not stumble.
Proverbs 3:23 (NASB)

Have you ever walked on uneven ground? You know the feeling…a little unstable and unsure you will make it across to a smoother surface? And if you have any knee issues like me, you also know how painful it can be when the ground you are walking on is less than flat.

Life can be that way too. Some days run smoothly. On other days, nothing seems to go right and it becomes total chaos. We then begin to feel unstable and unsure about what to do.

God says in Proverbs 3:21, *"My son* (daughter), *let them not depart from your sight; Keep sound wisdom and discretion."* And in Proverbs 2:6, He says, *"For the Lord gives wisdom; From His mouth come knowledge and understanding."*

The way to walk securely and not stumble is to "keep sound wisdom and discretion" and the One who *"gives wisdom and understanding"* is God. All we need to do is "think about Him in

all your (our) ways, and He will guide you (us) on the right paths."
(Proverbs 3:6)

If we begin our day without meeting God, we begin on uneven
ground. The result is instability with the risk of stumbling, falling
and pain. But if we meet with God first thing each morning, He
will guide our every step.

God promises to be with us through everything our day brings.
Even more, He has gone before us and knows how the day will go.

With that promise, we can have confidence by seeking Him
first, our paths will be clear and straight. The ground before us will
feel smooth and, though life will at times be bumpy, we will have
stability through any uneven ground life brings.

Heavenly Father, You are worthy of my first attention of the day. Thank You
that I can come to You each day and You will meet me and set my mind and
feet on even ground. Help me to remember that I have access to your wisdom
so my day will not be out of control but in your control. In Jesus' name,
amen.

Responding In Love

Rebecca Cleere

My dear brothers and sisters, take note of this: Everyone should be quick to
listen, slow to speak and slow to become angry, because human anger does
not produce
the righteousness that God desires.
James 1:19-20 (NIV)

Yikes! I don't know if you're like me, but I love the book of
James.

He is so direct and there is little to no room for misinterpretation.
These verses are etched in my mind and I have to call on them
more often then I care to admit. It seems so easy here in black and
white: listen then speak.

However, this is contrary to our "me-centered" culture. I think
the fact that James includes the words "slow to anger" indicates
that we are not always going to like the words that our ears hear.

I have two sisters, Rachel and Veronica. We are best friends.
We talk to each other all the time. I think I am a pretty good
listener but I always have a lot to say, too!

Sometimes, in my haste to make sure my thoughts are heard,

I may say something that hurts someone or sometimes it's vice versa. Regrettably, I can get upset if someone isn't willing to listen to me. That can lead to anger and, again, there in black and white it says my anger will NOT bring about the righteousness of God. That, my friends, is no good.

We must learn to control our way of responding versus reacting. Scripture is full of verses that talk about the way we treat each other. It just takes one scroll through someone's social media comments to see that "slow to speak and slow to become angry" is a response that is challenging to many people.

It is my belief that if we, you and me, will do what this verse is calling us to do, we will see radical changes in our relationships.

It is difficult to argue or fight with someone who is being patient, attentive and sensitive to your feelings.

Heavenly Father, open my ears to hear and truly listen and open my heart to respond in love. Lead me, Father, in the righteousness You desire. Amen.

The Promise Keeper

Rebecca Joy Hardin

For thus says the Lord: Even the captives of the mighty shall be taken, and the prey of the tyrant be rescued, for I will contend with those who contend with you, and I will save your children.
Isaiah 49:25 (ESV)

This is an amazing promise the Lord made to His people in Isaiah's time.

He also makes this promise to us today. When we put our faith in Jesus, we become His covenant people through His blood.

Whether we are single, married, a young adult or beautifully seasoned, we are the daughters of His heart whom He treasures. His love is upon us for He is our wonderful Promise Keeper.

Whatever we consecrate and surrender to Him, He's always faithful to honor.

I've been married fifty years and have two grown children and a twenty-year-old grandson. I can tell you about this Promise Keeper over and over again. He is amazing. His love never fails.

This particular verse is very personal to me. It's underlined so many times in my Bible that the ink has bled through to the other side. It also has our son's name Isaac written beside it.

There was a time when Isaac was in a serious spiritual battle, and I was burdened and concerned. I was worn out from intense prayer with many tears.

The Lord revealed to me that this verse was for our son and I surrendered him to Jesus. That was some time ago. Isaac is now soaring in Christ. His faith is strong, and he is living in his destiny.

Today, our entire family is serving Jesus together and we know the best is yet to come! Why? Because Jesus is our Promise Keeper – yesterday, today and forever. He is our rock! He is faithful and the love of our lives.

Dear Father, remind us always that You are our Promise Keeper. In Jesus' name, amen.

Seek God Instead Of His Goodies

Sharon Shelton

The Lord is my Shepherd (to feed, guide, and shield me),
I shall not lack.
Psalm 23:1 (AMP)

I have walked with the Lord for more than half my adult life. As I look back and reflect on His companionship, I am awe struck at how faithful He has been to shepherd me. He hasn't missed a lick!

When I've been sick, He's healed me. When I've been financially strapped, He's prospered me. When I've been struck down, He's raised me up. When I've been frightened, He's comforted me. When I've needed protection, He's shielded me. He's delivered me out of more fixes than one can imagine!

In reflecting on what a wonderful Shepherd He is, I am ashamed at how many times I have come whining instead of coming to brag on Him, telling Him to His face how good and wonderful He is.

Getting down to the bottom of *why* we worship and petition Him would eliminate a lot of soulish, childish utterances. Prayers where the mindset behind them scream, "I am a child of God; therefore, I deserve to have" … or "I'm the head and not the tail; therefore, I deserve to have the most successful and prosperous business than all of our competitors." (Yep. I've been guilty of this: Seeking the goodies instead of God).

We all want the blessings of Jesus Christ. We all want Him to give us a better life. But as a dear pastor once said, "If we embrace the Lord in order to have a better life, we've missed it. That is idolatry. We embrace the Lord Jesus because He is worthy." Period.

Thank You, Heavenly Father, for being my Shepherd and Provider in my time of need. In Jesus' name, amen.

The Gift Of Singleness

Sloane Keith

And the single woman is focused on the things of the Lord so she can be holy both in body and spirit. But a married woman is concerned about the things of the world and how she may please her husband. I am trying to help you and make things easier for you and not make things difficult, but so that you would have undistracted devotion, serving the Lord constantly with an undivided heart.

1 Corinthians 7:34-35 (TPT)

For decades, being single has had a negative stigma. Rather, we can choose to see it as a great adventure, instead of a curse for women who are anxiously waiting for the day they will meet their prince charming.

However, we single women need to change this negative image of being single. Instead of seeing it as a curse, let's look at it with a different lens and realize it can be a gift from God.

As it says in these Scriptures, the gift is "that you would have undistracted devotion, serving the Lord constantly with an undivided heart." Hence, when we are single, we have more time to know Him and His character, more time to serve Him and His people and more time for Him in this season than we will have after marriage.

I want to challenge and encourage you, dear waiting friend, to use this time of singleness to seek God's face and realize that He, and not marriage, is your true destiny. You will find unspeakable joy in serving the Lord and, in time, I believe He will bless you with that amazing man of God.

Lord, please help me to see being single as the gift that it is. Help me to find my contentment and joy in You in this season. Grow and mold me into the woman of God You have called me to be.
In Jesus' name, amen.

Overcoming Fear

Tabitha May-DeBoer

For God has not given us a spirit of fear, but of power and of love and of a sound mind.
2 Timothy 1:7 (NKJV)

How do you decide when fear, instead of God, is guiding you? In stressful situations, it becomes difficult to decipher healthy from unhealthy fear. The two can feel the same but healthy fear is totally different. In my experience, most people who seek prayer or counseling struggle with this one thing: fear.

Fear is the opposite of faith, but at times it feels the same as faith. The dilemma is that it hides within us as a false truth. When it speaks to our heart, it has one goal – to convince us a lie is a truth. Fear whispers in our ears, "You can't do it, you aren't good enough, you will fail." Every time we confront the boundaries of our spiritual walk, fear will try to keep us from growing in the faith.

In this particular verse, God shows you how to overcome fear. He tells you in the first phrase that He "has not given us a spirit of fear" even when you face a battle.

The next phrase – "but of power and of love" – reveals the resources He has for you. God knows your earthly labor to stay free from fear requires power.

No one wants to be empty-handed without God's power. And you need His power to declare and decree the Word over your circumstances. Then, the love that He gives you covers your fear of inadequacy. You can learn that nothing changes His feelings or plans for you.

Lastly, God gives you a sound mind that is the culmination of power and love. These two ingredients are the recipe for security. When you have the power to face the battle and the love to accept the struggle, you have a plan for overcoming fear and producing stable growth.

God, is there a place in my heart where fear has guided me? Remove fear and guide me with your power and love. Forgive me for doubting my security in You. Take my whole heart and I will trust You.
In Jesus' name, amen.

The Impossible

Vivian Fernand Narcisse

Don't be afraid, for I am with you. Don't be discouraged, for I am your God.
I will strengthen you and help you. I will hold you up with my victorious
right hand.
Isaiah 41:10 (NLT)

My sisters, have you ever felt like you were facing a tremendous or impossible task?

Have you ever thought you did not have the ability, intelligence or courage to complete a job/assignment you were called to do?

If you answered "yes" to any of these questions, you are surely not alone. Welcome to the family of the "Impossible."

Several years ago, when I was pursuing my Ph.D., there were times when I felt the task was too much for me and I wanted to give up. This was especially true at the beginning of my studies as I adjusted to the amount of work and the high expectations that are put on a Ph.D. student.

Throughout my graduate education, I asked God to help me successfully complete my studies and He did. During this season of my life, I learned what it meant to trust in the Lord with all my heart and not to depend on my own understanding. (Proverbs 3:5)

The Lord may place you in challenging and seemingly impossible circumstances for you to learn to trust Him. When that happens, He wants you to depend totally on Him to complete the task.

Therefore, as we surrender to God, He equips us to successfully achieve our mission. He tells us that we need not fear or be discouraged because He is with us and is our God. He promised to strengthen, help us and to give us victory! Whatever we accomplish in this life is through His grace and mercy.

Father, I will trust You in all my ways. Give me the courage, strength, wisdom and ability to face any situation in life especially those that seem challenging to me. Thank you for being the God of the impossible. In Jesus' name, amen.

In Agreement

Vivian Bustillos Keith

*Again I say to you that if two of you agree on earth concerning anything
that they ask, it will be done for them
by My Father in heaven.
Matthew 18:19 (NKJV)*

I remember the day my husband Bill gave me my first Spirit Filled Life Bible and I couldn't wait to get my hands on it. It was filled with many study tools like the Word Wealth section which caught my eye immediately! This section has the English meanings of original Greek and Hebrew words along with helpful insights. And I love to delve into the meaning of words.

When I came upon this particular verse, I was intrigued with the word "agree" which is *sumphoneo* in Greek. *Sumphoneo* means to sound together, to be in accord, be in harmony. Quite interesting, the word "symphony" comes from this Greek word.

As I meditated on this particular word, it took me back to my band class in junior high school. It was customary at the start of the class for everyone to tune their instruments by the playing a certain key in unison in order to play the songs in perfect harmony.

This memory reminded me the importance of being in agreement with other believers in our Christian walk.

In the spiritual realm, if we harmonize (agree) and ask anything of the Father, He will do it. As we pray in agreement, He ignites and manifests His great power. Don't you know how it pleases the Lord when we go to Him and ask Him to do the impossible? He loves us and desires to answer our prayers.

In 2017, my son Miguel was diagnosed with an aggressive form of nasal cancer. I reached out to a host of Christian families and friends to agree with me that my son would live not die and proclaim the works of the Lord (Psalm 118:17). God heard our prayers and today Miguel is a walking testimony of God's healing power. God is good and worthy to be praised!

Father, thank You for your Word that is alive and full of power. Help us to always seek You first in all things and to be in agreement with your Word without fear, anxiety or dismay and believing all things are possible with You. In Jesus' name, amen.

Worship

Allison Wolfe Cunningham

Therefore, I urge you, brothers, in view of God's mercy, to offer your bodies as living sacrifices, holy and pleasing to God – this is your reasonable act of worship.
Romans 12:1 (NIV)

It is a fascinating concept that when Christ's followers come together, He manifests His presence in their midst and meets people personally.

Corporate expression of worship is powerful and energizing yet it still comes down to one to one ratio. It is not a spectator thing reserved to a specific place and time. It's giving honor, devotion and your heart's affection to the One who is worthy.

This requires time spent with Jesus. Worship is the opportunity to sit at the King's feet and behold him. To know his heart. To see his beauty. At the King's feet, you realize His affirmation and love in your innermost being as every part of you is satisfied.

Time spent in God's presence empowers you to worship Him in daily living. Because Christ laid down His life, you surrender your life to Him.

Worship is clapping your hands, dancing, singing a song, preferring others over yourself, giving to the poor...worship is more than music.

It's a heart posture that exalts Jesus and is demonstrated in the words of your mouth and fruit of your life. There is no distinction between spiritual and secular in the Kingdom of God. Life in God's kingdom requires living unto the King in the attitude of your heart and in the work of your hands.

A living sacrifice sounds counterintuitive yet it's an invitation to worship the Father by yielding your will and priorities at the feet of Jesus knowing He is worthy of everything you are!

God, help me to prioritize my life to create space for one on one time with You. Give me courage to worship You with the expression of my words motivated by a pure heart that offers up a living sacrifice of a life that pleases You. Amen.

Wedding Day

Patricia Binkley-Childress

*I will rejoice greatly in the Lord, My soul will exult in my God; For He
has clothed me with garments of salvation, He has wrapped me with a robe
of righteousness, As a bridegroom decks himself with a garland, And as a
bride adorns herself
with her jewels.
Isaiah 61:10 (NASB)*

Every young girl dreams of her wedding day and the prince that will whisk her away to a castle where life will be a fairy tale filled with love, laughter and family.

From engagement to wedding day, we joyfully anticipate the moment of the "I do's" and the beginning our lives with the man of our dreams.

Ten years later, we're knee deep in laundry, chores, sick and very active children, and two careers that barely leave room for time with our prince. We start wondering what happened to the joy we felt on our wedding day. When life gets clouded with repetitive day-to-day tasks, we then begin to daydream about a less serious time in life.

All wives experience times when it feels like the "honeymoon is over." When we expect our husbands to be the source of our joy, life will creep in and steal it. But when we expect our joy to come from God, remember what He did on the cross and the "Wedding Day" we will experience when we reach Heaven, every day will be filled with joy, excitement and hope!

We're all guilty of expecting our marriage to bring us joy, yet God is the only one who can accomplish that. "You make known to me the path of life; in Your presence there is fullness of joy; at Your right hand are pleasures forevermore." (Psalm 16:11)

It is in those times when life is real that we need to remind ourselves of whose bride we really are. Only then will our joy be everlasting and complete.

Precious Father, forgive me for expecting my joy to come only from my husband. Thank You for giving him to me but help me to remember that my joy is complete in You and You alone. And help me to fully understand that I am your bride and one day I will be with You on OUR Wedding day! In Jesus' name. amen.

God Listens

Vivian Bustillos Keith

The LORD has heard my supplication,
The LORD receives my prayer.
Psalm. 6:9 (NASB)

How comforting it is to know the Lord hears and receives our prayers. We don't have to make an appointment with Him, call Him on our cell phone or send Him a text message or email.

No matter what our spiritual condition, nothing can hold God back from leaning His ear to us. The moment we call out to Him, He shows up without delay.

In my early Christian years, I had this "stinking thinking" mentality that God did not listen to or answer my prayers. Either I didn't get what I was asking for within a certain time frame or I thought God was punishing me for something I did or said. Little did I know that God was either saying, "No, Vivian, not now," He was protecting me, or maybe it was not His will at that time for me to receive what I was asking.

Psalm 66:19 says, *"But truly God has listened; he has attended to the voice of my prayer."* We can be encouraged that not only has

He heard our prayers, but He has dealt with them. Though we are not capable of seeing things through God's eyes and we may not accept His answer, we have to remember that He will care for us and we can trust Him with our lives.

To believe that God wants the very best for us is an indication we can trust Him. We should not make any provision for fear, doubt or unbelief to enter our minds during our prayer time. Instead, let us be confident that the One who created us in our mother's womb and called us by name before the beginning of time, takes pleasure in receiving and answering our prayers.

During the thirty-eight years I have walked with the Lord, I strived to pray the Father's will rather than to persuade Him to see things my way. Our God is a loving Father who delights in giving what is best for His children, which is why we pray with confidence knowing that He hears our prayers.

Heavenly Father, thank You that You hear our supplications.
We praise You for receiving our prayers and meeting our needs. Amen.

The Authors

Alaina Strait is married to Mark and they have two amazing kids. She works as an accounting administrative assistant in Longview. She attends Pathway Church where her husband is the executive pastor and she serves on the Women and Children's Ministry leadership team.

Allison Wolfe Cunningham is passionate about Jesus and His Word. Wherever she goes, the love of God overflows from Allison's life. She is a wife and mother of three teenage children as well as a licensed minister, speaker and mentor.

Andrée Elliott accepted Jesus as her Savior in 1976. She earned her doctorate degree in Molecular Biology from Texas Woman's University and was a university professor (1989-2016). She currently is the owner and chief research scientist of Bezalel Lab in Longview.

Beth Collins serves on the worship team at Gateway Church in Southlake. She has a passion to see people connect with God through intimate praise and worship and receive healing during worship. She is married to Clay and they have four children.

Brenda Telles has been married for twenty-seven years and has two sons. She attended the School of Ministry, Church of the Open Door in Waco and is on the national board of Women of Worship Ministry in Florida. She is passionate about telling others of God's saving grace.

Christine Lanton lives in Texas with her husband of thirty-two years. She loves spending time with ther children and grandchildren. She is an advocate for God, the Bible, the truth, and many important political and social causes.

Dawana Quintana was born into a pastor's home and attended Christ for the Nations Institute. In Dallas. She has served in various ministries, including overseas missionary service. She is happily married to Frank Quintana and is the mother of three extraordinary children.

DeAnna Lucas is a twenty-four year old go-getter. She obtained her degree in Youth Ministry from Christ for the Nations Institute in Dallas. Upon graduating she then took her adventures across the ocean to Warrington, England, to work along side Hope Church Warrington.

Debbie Lucas is married to Michael and they have four grown children and one granddaughter. She served in many areas of ministry for over thirty years. She is currently the Leader of the Women's Ministry at The Church of Garden Valley.

Deena Shelton, PhD, is a licensed professional counselor supervisor in East Texas. She loves spending time with her husband and two children. In her spare time, she volunteers in her community and looks for ways to empower others to reach their goals and dreams.

Diane Hawkins is a wife, mother, sister, friend and mentor. She has two daughters, one son and is a grandmother to four granddaughters. She and her husband reside in Longview and she enjoys reading and researching Christian history in her spare time.

Elsa Guajardo has traveled her native state of Texas as a PK (preacher's kid) but is a longtime resident of Fort Worth. She and her husband Ramon have three wonderful children and three grandsons. She prays each day that the Lord will use it to glorify His name.

Helen Lynn has been faithfully led by the Lord for over forty years. She has experienced the height, breath, length and depth of His un-surpassing love, mercy and grace. Her greatest joy is watching her three children and five grandchildren walk in truth found in the Word of God.

Holly Frank believes that there is purpose to every part of life. She loves that Jesus is ready to give freely. She's a mom of boys who somehow all turned out to be as strong-willed and wild as they are handsome. She and her husband live in North Carolina.

Janie Peña has been a Christian for many years and is a member at Crosspoint Church in McKinney. She served at Primera Iglesia Bautista for thirty-five years, taught Sunday school and served on several committees. She enjoyed a career in education and external affairs.

Jenn Eze is a lover of Christ, wife and mother of four children. She owns a web design company and lives in Oklahoma. She is a passionate and prophetic voice. She lives her life to be simply a sign pointing to The Way, The Truth and The Life - Yeshua!

Jessica Wilson is an associate pastor at Pathway Church in Longview. She is passionate about helping women and children discover who they are in Christ and grow in their relationship with Him. Jessica and her husband Paul have two beautiful kids Wyatt and Lauryn Kate.

Julia Lutz grew up in Quanah. She is an RN, MSN and the mother to Micah married to Ashley and Heather married to Matt. She has two wonderful grandchildren. She received Jesus at the age of twelve. She has served in numerous ministries throughout her Christian walk.

Kelly Mays works as a customer service representative. She enjoys summertime and spending time outdoors with family and friends. She is an avid coffee drinker, self-professed comedian and child of God.

Linda Serrano is singer/songwriter/organist and minister of the Word. She has served the Lord from a young age. She is happily married to Osiel Serrano and together they have two wonderful children, Osiel Jr. and Jacob, and one granddaughter, Layla.

Lucie Grove is a lover of Jesus and widow of retired Lt. Col. Daniel M. Grove (USAF) who was pastor of Mooringsport United Methodist Church in Lousiana. She currently works as a hospice RN. She has two sons who live in Heaven, one daughter and four grandchildren.

Maimuna Abeh has been married to Abel Mbeh, a wonderful man of God, for twenty-two years and they have three amazing daughters. Maimuna has been a Christian since 2008. She currently attends Pathway Church in Longview and leads a women's prayer group.

Mary Mendez grew up in Lancaster in the early 60's. She received her bachelors of arts degree from SMU and has been an educator since 1984 as a teacher/coach. She currently teaches in Grand Prairie. She is the mother of two adult children and a grandmother of three.

Maye Moore is an ambassador of Christ from Vivian, Louisiana. She has been saved for fifty years and ministers in praise and worship and intercession. She is a wife, mother and a nana.

Natalia Meltabarger is an aspiring author and inspirational speaker with a bachelor's of science degree from Southwestern Assemblies of God University in Waxahachie. She is married to Mark and they have three sons and a little Yorkshire terrier.

Pat Lewis has been married to Maj. Gen. (Ret.) Vernon B. Lewis Jr. for sixty-six years. She is the mother of three, grandmother of four and great grandmother of little Franny to be born in the spring. A retired RN who loves the Lord, she has made numerous mission trips to Israel.

Patricia Childress currently works with her husband, Dr. Carl Childress. She is the mother of five, a grandmother of five and great-grandmother of one. She considers sharing her faith with the lost and encouraging fellow Christians to be her greatest privilege.

Rachel Wilson is a mom of four children, wife to Craig and a second-grade teacher. She also leads worship at her church. Rachel lives in Rowlett and loves spending time with her friends and family.

Rebecca Cleere is a native of Garland. She lives with her sweet husband Seth and two children Caleb and Lydia. She is a member of Freeman Heights Baptist Church and serves in several ministries. Her passion is singing and loves to spend time with her family.

Rebecca Joy Hardin has been married to Jim for fifty years. They have ministered together for many years in pastoral care. She is gifted as an intercessor, encourager and psalmist. Today, they are on the serve team at Pathway Church in Longview.

Rhonda Baker lives with her husband and children in Gilmer. She is a graduate of Texas A&M University and has been serving in the public-school system as an educator for almost twenty years. Rhonda holds fast to God's Word, believing it to be God-breathed and inerrant.

Sharon Shelton is the wife of forty-seven years to Robert Shelton. They have two children and four grandchildren. She has been in the faith since 1981 when she received a divine healing and the baptism of the Holy Spirit. She has led Bible studies and mentored young women.

Sherry Bridwell became a Christian at the age of eight years old. She is a member of Pathway Church in Longview. She has been married to Lance for forty-eight years who was her school sweetheart since the fourth grade. Sherry has two adult children and two grandchildren.

Sloane Keith is an eighth grade English teacher in Shreveport, Louisiana. She enjoys writing, hanging out with friends, and drinking lots of coffee! Her passion is to help young women grow in the Lord despite the many pressures the world places on them.

Tabitha May-DeBoer is an ordained minister and a certified faith-based counselor. She and her husband Gary together have eight children and six grandchildren. She is the founder of "The Elephant's Roost" which helps people walk in the freedom in Christ.

Tara Keith Hickman was born in Tokyo, Japan, to missionary parents. She and her late husband raised two incredible children and now she has two grandchildren. She and her husband Chohn live in Burleson and attend Cana Baptist Church.

Vivian Fernand Narcisse chose to follow Jesus Christ thirty-two years ago in Suriname, South America. She is an associate professor of chemistry at Palm Beach Atlantic University in Florida. She is married to Serge and they attend Family Church Village.

Vivian Bustillos Keith is an ordained minister and has been a follower of Christ for thirty-eight years. She is married to author Bill Keith and they attend Church on the Rock in Lubbock. She has a passion to pray for others and enjoys Greek word studies.

Made in the USA
Coppell, TX
09 March 2021

51479492R00132